D1491745

THE STORY OF
THE PRAYER BOOK

THE BIBLE IN ENGLISH, 15TH CENTURY

Fresco in St. Stephen's Hall in the British Houses of Parliament, by George Clausen, R.A.
Under the picture is inscribed: 'The English people, in spite of persecution for heresy, persist
in gathering secretly to read aloud Wycliffe's English Bible.'

THE STORY OF
THE PRAYER BOOK

IN THE OLD AND NEW WORLD
AND THROUGHOUT THE
ANGLICAN CHURCH

By

PERCY DEARMER

Based upon the Author's
EVERYMAN'S HISTORY OF THE
PRAYER BOOK

WITH 97
ILLUSTRATIONS

LONDON
OXFORD UNIVERSITY PRESS
NEW YORK TORONTO

Oxford University Press, Amen House, London E.C.4

GLASGOW NEW YORK TORONTO MELBOURNE WELLINGTON
BOMBAY CALCUTTA MADRAS KARACHI KUALA LUMPUR
CAPE TOWN IBADAN NAIROBI ACCRA

First edition 1933
Reprinted 1940, 1948, 1950, 1953 and 1958

PRINTED IN GREAT BRITAIN

PREFACE

A NEW and shorter name is now given to this book, because it has been in great part rewritten—revised in the light of recent knowledge and expanded to meet the requirements of the whole Anglican Church, that great, free, and reconciling Communion which has spread and developed in so remarkable a way during the twenty years that have elapsed since *Everyman's History of the Prayer Book* was first published.

The writer owes special gratitude to the friends who helped him in his work, particularly to Dr. W. H. Frere, Bishop of Truro, and to the late Dr. Brightman, who carefully worked through the whole original manuscript and the proofs in 1912. Permission was graciously given by Queen Alexandra to reproduce Professor Tuxen's picture of a beautiful incident in the Coronation Service of 1902, Fig. 10 in this book. The author is also much indebted to many who have helped him in providing other illustrations. Those who wish to study further the origins of the Prayer Book will find in Brightman's *The English Rite* (Rivingtons, 1915) the complete texts of the Books of 1549, 1552, and 1662, printed in parallel columns, while the sources are detailed at the side.

The cover of the book was designed by Mr. George Kruger Grey.

1933

CONTENTS

LIST OF ILLUSTRATIONS

PART I
THE MATERIAL OF PUBLIC WORSHIP

CHAPTER I

THE BIBLE IN THE PRAYER BOOK

THERE are two Books in the English language which stand out pre-eminent above all others, which are better known and more important even than the works of our greatest poets. They are the Bible and the Book of Common Prayer. We may, indeed, regard the Bible as within the Prayer Book; since the Prayer Book, in its Table of Lessons, arranges for the Bible as a whole to be read through, day by day, once in the year, and thus a Bible is as necessary for the conduct of Divine Service as a Prayer Book. Moreover, the Prayer Book itself contains the whole Psalter (taken, not from the Authorized Version of 1611, but from the Great Bible of 1540), as well as that ancient collection of passages from the New Testament (with a few from the Old) called the Epistles and Gospels for the Communion Service.

The theology also and the thought of the Prayer Book are everywhere in much closer conformity with the teaching of the New Testament—than the other historical liturgies, which date from about the 5th century; and the second preface, 'Concerning the Service of the Church' (which was the original preface of the First English Prayer Book), bases the whole Reformation, so far as the Divine Service was concerned, upon the need of daily Bible reading in the mother tongue at 'the Common Prayers in the Church'. This, the preface says, was the method of the ancient Fathers, who so ordered the matter that—

'all the whole Bible, (or the greatest part thereof) should be read over once every year; intending thereby, that the Clergy, and especially such as were Ministers in the congregation, should (by often reading, and meditation in God's Word) be stirred up to godliness themselves, and be more able to exhort

others by wholesome doctrine, and to confute them that were
adversaries to the truth; and further, that the people (by

1. THE TITLE OF ST. LUKE'S GOSPEL
A page from a 9th-century Gospel Book.

daily hearing of Holy Scripture read in the Church) might
continually profit more and more in the knowledge of God,
and be the more inflamed with the love of his true religion'.

Thus the Divine Service of the Anglican Churches is based

upon the principle of daily Bible-reading in the house of God. On Sundays the more important passages in the Scriptures are selected in the Lessons as well as in the Epistles and Gospels, and now in the Psalter also.

Our Book, then, is an instrument of the Bible, and, as it were, a framework to the Bible, carrying with itself the whole Scriptures into the service of the Church. Thus the Bible is given a place supreme, as the sacred library of the Christian revelation. It is the greatest book in the world; but next to it, among English books, the English-speaking peoples would probably place the Book of Common Prayer and Shakespeare. That is to say, we have in all the churches and chapels of the Anglican Church[1]— from New Zealand to the Himalaya, from Alaska to the Cape of Good Hope—two supreme books in common daily use.

Yet, in its very ordering of the Bible, the Prayer Book protects us against that unintelligent jumbling together of the Old and New Testaments which has caused so many people to doubt the Christian revelation altogether. By our use of the Bible in Church we are reminded every day that it is a collection of books, some of which have a higher value than others, while the New Testament holds a position markedly different from that of the Old. Certain parts of the Old Testament are frankly put aside as not suitable for Church reading at all, while the sublimest passages are read twice, thrice, or even four times a year, and the Psalms are said or sung twelve times. Again, whereas the Old Testament as a whole is read through once a year, the New

[1] Here, for the sake of clearness, in the first and last footnote of this book, let me say that the terms 'Anglican Church' and the less euphonious 'Anglican Communion' mean the mother Church of England together with all the other Churches, such as the Episcopal Churches of America and Scotland, which are in the same communion. In like manner the Eastern Orthodox Church includes the Churches of Greece, Russia, Serbia, and the other Churches in that Communion. A list of these Anglican Churches is given on p. 17.

Testament is read twice; and at the Holy Communion the New Testament is read almost exclusively. Nor is there wanting even here an important distinction: the most precious part of the whole Bible, the record of our Lord's deeds and sayings in the four Gospels, is marked (in accordance with very ancient custom) by special ceremonial, and all the people stand; whereas, when the letters of the Apostles are read in the Epistle for the day, the people sit.

CHAPTER II

THE QUESTION OF SET FORMS OF PRAYER

THIS noble liturgical heritage has not come down to us without many struggles. Nowadays, though there are still parties and prejudices in the Christian Church, yet sensible Churchmen of all schools agree in their devotion to the Book of Common Prayer—even those who neglect to carry out many of its directions; and our brothers also of the Free Churches do in great measure regard the Prayer Book as a heritage which they possess in common with us. We are glad that it should be so; we are glad to see that they use it more and more, so that their services are permeated with its noble phrases, while in some of their churches the appointed forms of worship are almost indistinguishable from our own.

But it was not always so. A movement arose in the 16th century, which threatened the very existence of liturgical services, and which indeed triumphed during those fifteen years of Cromwellian absolutism, when Parliament was silenced and England governed by a military dictatorship. The use of the Prayer Book was forbidden by law from 1645 till the Restoration in 1660, and its place was taken by the Directory for Public Worship, which gave only general directions as to what the minister was to do. The opposition to ordered forms of liturgical worship grew in intensity, and the time came when some Presbyterians in Scotland (who had at first used the Genevan 'Book of Common Order') would not even say the Lord's Prayer, because it was a set form. During the last half-century Scottish Presbyterians have been successfully reviving the use of liturgical services; but none the less there are still many people all over the world who prefer extemporary prayer.

It is worth while, therefore, asking ourselves at the outset, Is liturgical worship a good thing, or ought the minister to make up his own prayers?

Now, there is very much to be said for extemporaneous worship in church; it certainly should have a place in all Churches, and not for mission work alone. It secures the necessary element of freedom; furthermore, it may bring spontaneity and vitality into a service, and is a good corrective of formalism.

Indeed, not only must Free Services quite independent of any fixed forms (except for the hymns) have their place in every live part of the Christian Church, but the free element exists also within the liturgical services themselves. The Prone is as old as the Church of England, and it has been forgotten: even its more formal expression, the Bidding Prayer, was almost given up during the liturgical chaos of the Victorian era. Yet the Prone supplies just that free element which quickens and expands the traditional services: the minister stands in the pulpit and offers prayer in his own way; and for this he is not confined to the splendid phrases of the Bidding Prayer, but is free to use the briefest of biddings, saying merely, 'Let us pray for . . .' (following, it may be, with a versicle and response), and using for each moment of prayer either silence, or a short prayer of his own making, or a collect. As Dr. Brightman said in his Preface to *The English Rite*, 'We often hear that "elasticity" is needed'; but it generally turns out that the elasticity contemplated 'is only a choice of rigidities'; and the Prone gives us just the needed elasticity. When it precedes the sermon, a hymn may be sung between the two, as indeed is always done when the Prone takes the now common form of prayers said after the anthem (or corresponding hymn), the minister standing at the west end of the church.

Nor is there anything alien to Church ways or wrong in

principle about extempore services. Indeed as late as the 4th century the celebrant at the Eucharist used still to pray thus. The service went on certain general lines, but the 'president' filled it in according to his own ideas, and offered up 'prayers and thanksgivings with all his strength', the people saying 'Amen' (as is told on p. 194). It was only by degrees that the prayers thus offered became fixed. Liturgical worship was a gradual development.

We can perhaps realize best the objections to regular extemporaneous worship if we quote the greatest English defender of it, John Milton. Ah! if only he had been on the other side, what matchless collects he might have added to the Prayer Book at the Restoration! Now Milton objected to a

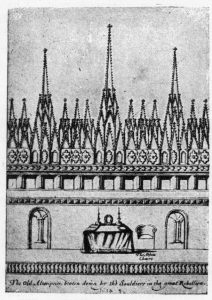

2. BEFORE THE PRAYER BOOK WAS PUT DOWN

The altar and screen of Peterborough Cathedral, destroyed by the Puritan soldiers in 1643.

liturgy because he thought it a slur upon the extemporary powers of the minister: 'Well may men of eminent gifts', he wrote, 'set forth as many forms and helps to prayer as they please; but to impose them on ministers lawfully called and sufficiently tried ... is a supercilious tyranny, impropriating the Spirit of God to themselves.' On which Professor Raleigh dryly comments: 'Milton, we know, did not habitually attend public worship at any of the conventicles of the sectaries, or perhaps he might have found reason to modify this censure.'

Milton's mistake was, in fact, a very simple one. He thought that every minister would be a Milton. He did not realize what a deadly thing average custom can be, what a deadly bore an average man can make of himself when compelled to do continually a thing for which he has no natural gift. He did not foresee the insidious danger of unreality and cant. We should all, of course, flock to hear Milton praying extempore, if he were to come to this life again; but there are many mute, inglorious ministers whom we would rather not hear.

To put all the prayers as well as the sermon in the hands of the officiating minister is indeed a form of sacerdotalism which the Church most wisely rejected many centuries ago. We know what a joy and help it would be to hear an inspired saint, with a genius for rapid prose composition, make up prayers as he went along; and opportunities for extemporization do exist, as we have said, outside the appointed services. But the Church has to provide for the average man, and has to guard against that form of clerical absolutism which would put a congregation at the mercy of the idiosyncrasies and shortcomings of one person. For extempore services, which should be a safeguard for freedom, can easily degenerate into a tyranny.

There is, let it be admitted, a certain loss in always having very familiar prayers; and if there has been formalism in extempore prayer, there has too often been an even worse formalism in the use of the Prayer Book. Indeed it is no mere paradox to say that the service least in danger of formalism is that which is rich in outward forms; for history and a wide knowledge of Christendom show us that good ceremonies are a great preservative against Pharisaism. The reason for this is that action, music, colour, form, sight, scent, and sound appeal more freely to the individual worshipper, and more subtly, relieving the pressure of a rigid phraseology, and allowing the spirit many ways of rising up to God, unhampered by the accent of the workaday voice of man.

Thus, while we must secure the treasure of comprehensiveness by having a place both for spontaneous prayer and for those quiet meetings of silence which have given such a deep strength to Quakerism, we may be confident that liturgical worship is the best of all. There is some loss in the use of printed words; but there is a greater gain. We have in them the accumulated wisdom and beauty of the Christian Church, the garnered excellence of many saints. We are by them released from the accidents of time and place. Above all, we are preserved against the worst dangers of selfishness: in the common prayer we join together in a great fellowship that is as wide as the world; and we are guided, not by the limited notions of our own minister, nor by the narrow impulses of our own desires, but by the mighty voice that rises from the general heart of Christendom.

Our Lord had the ancient forms of the Church in which he lived often on his lips, and in the moment of his supreme agony it was a liturgical sentence, a fragment of the familiar service, that was wrung from him—'My God, my God, why hast thou forsaken me?' We have a richer heritage, for it is a heritage dowered by his Spirit; and from our treasure-house come things new and old. We love the old indeed; yet will we not forget the new. We will try to avoid the danger so common still among us, of being only able to pray by the book; remembering that there is a place and a real use for extemporary prayer, and a still greater use for the silent prayer which is above words altogether. These very things will keep fresh and sweet for us those old set forms, in which we can join so well because we know beforehand what they are about, and in which for the same reason all the people can come together in the fellowship of common prayer.

CHAPTER III

THE CONTENTS OF THE PRAYER BOOK

NOW that we have pointed out how the Bible is as much a service book of the Anglican Churches as the Book of Common Prayer, and have explained why it is a good thing to have printed forms of worship, we are ready to look at the Prayer Book as a whole. What *is* the Prayer Book?

We naturally turn to the Title-page and the Prefaces for our answer. Now the Title-page is a full and descriptive one; and at the very outset it removes a common mistake. It makes no mention of the Thirty-nine Articles; for they form no part of the Prayer Book. They are bound up with it, just as hymn-books often are; but no layman is required to give his assent to them. They are admirable in many ways, comprehensive and moderate, though written in an age of bitter controversy; but it would be absurd to suppose that they could not be improved after the discoveries and experience of nearly four centuries. Nothing has been done to improve them, except, in America after the Revolution, by the omission of Article 21 and the addition of a note to Article 35. The needs of modern thought have indeed been partly met in England since 1865 by altering the terms in which the clergy (and they alone) have to give what is now called their 'assent'; but this does not help the average man, who, moreover, is without the assistance of the learned commentaries which alone can prevent serious misunderstandings. In America the Articles are printed with the Prayer Book; but neither clergy nor laity are required to give formal assent to all their details.

The Title-page, then, in the first place reminds us that certain familiar things are only appendixes added to the Prayer Book— the State Services (in the English and Scottish Books), the

Articles, the Table of Kindred and Affinity, not to mention the Canons of 1603, and the Metrical Psalms which used to be bound up with the Prayer Book until our modern hymn-books drove them out of use.

To pass from the negative teaching of the Title-page, we find that it describes the Prayer Book as consisting of five parts —we may indeed rightly call them five books. Here is the Title-page of the present English Book (1662):

(1) *The Book of Common Prayer*
(2) *And Administration of the Sacraments,*
(3) *And other Rites and Ceremonies of the Church*
     according to the use of the Church of England
(4) *Together with the Psalter or Psalms of David*
     pointed as they are to be sung or said in Churches
(5) *And the Form and Manner of Making, Ordaining, and Consecrating* of Bishops, Priests, and Deacons.

The Prayer Book, then, consists of five books containing twenty-eight parts in England and twenty-nine in America. We give the numbers as they are in the Book Annexed to the Act of 1662, thus:

Book 1. THE BOOK OF COMMON PRAYER. The 'Common Prayer' is the name for those services which are conducted in the *choir* and at the *lectern*, (10) *Morning Prayer* and (11) *Evening Prayer*, which are therefore called choir services. There were formerly eight such services (see p. 157), and to-gether they are called the Divine Service. Common Prayer also includes (13) *The Litany*, which is traditionally a service of Intercession after Morning Prayer, before the Communion.

Book 2. ADMINISTRATION OF THE SACRAMENTS. (16) *Holy Communion* at the Lord's *Table*, and (17, 18) *Baptism*, at the *font*. In these Sacraments—outward signs of an inward grace—something is *done*: at the altar Christians receive the Communion; at the font non-Christians are admitted into the

Catholic or Universal Church. There are other outward signs in which something is done, as Confirmation, Matrimony, and Orders (the Ordination of Ministers); but there was much disputing at the time when the Prayer Book was produced as to the number of the Sacraments, and the English Church therefore contented herself with laying stress on the two great Sacraments of the Gospel, as they are called, Baptism and the holy Communion, leaving the 'five commonly called Sacraments, that is to say, Confirmation, Penance, Orders, Matrimony, and extreme Unction', in a separate category. There can be little doubt that this was the wisest way of settling an unhappy and precarious dispute.

Between these two books of Common Prayer and of the Sacraments there are printed in the Book of 1662, besides the Litany: (12) for use 'At Morning Prayer', the Confession of Faith 'commonly [but inaccurately] called the *Creed of Saint Athanasius*'; (14) The '*Prayers and Thanksgivings* upon several occasions', which are used both in the Divine Service and in the Litany, and therefore are conveniently printed here; (15) '*The Collects, Epistles, and Gospels* to be used at the Ministration of the holy Communion, throughout the year', as they are described in the Table of Contents; the Collects, however, are used also at Mattins and Evensong. In the American and in the Irish Books the Collects, &c., are printed after the Communion Service; and there are other differences in the order.

Book 3. OTHER RITES AND CEREMONIES OF THE CHURCH. It will be noticed that both the Sacraments and the 'other' Rites are described as 'of the Church', services, that is to say, not of the Anglican Church only, but of the whole Church; though their ritual (i.e. the manner of *saying*) and their ceremonial (i.e. the manner of *doing*) are according to the Anglican Use. Furthermore, the Title-page does not say 'All other Rites'; there are some which are not in the Prayer Book (p. 120), such as, in

3. LECTERN, PULPIT, CHOIR, AND ALTAR
Wookey Church, Somerset.

An old church; but the lectern, pulpit, choir, screen, and altar, as well as the decoration of the ceiling were made in 1923 by Mr. F. E. Howard for the Warham Guild.

England, the Coronation Service, or the Form for the Consecration of a Church, which are used under episcopal sanction; but the other Churches of our Communion include this latter service in their Prayer Books.

These Rites consist of certain of the 'five commonly called Sacraments', namely (19) *Confirmation*, to which is prefixed the *Catechism*, which is the preparation for Confirmation, and was only separated from it at the last Revision; and in the American Book *The Office of Instruction*; (20) the *Solemnization of Matrimony*; and (21) the *Visitation and Communion of the Sick*.

Then follow other Rites in the Book of 1662, (22) the Order for the *Burial of the Dead*, (23) the Churching, or *Thanksgiving of Women after Child-birth*, and (24) the Ash Wednesday service called *A Commination*. Other services in the American, Canadian, Irish, and Scottish Books are mentioned on pp. 142–5.

Book 4. THE PSALTER. The complete Book of the Psalms (26) which form the most essential part of Mattins and Evensong; they are arranged to be 'read through once every month', by grouping them under Morning and Evening Prayer for thirty days.

In 1662 two sets of services had been added—(17) the *Order of Baptism for those of Riper Years* (18), and (26) the *Forms of Prayer to be used at Sea*. The latter were inserted after the Psalter: it was doubtless felt that these sea services could not in the main be classed under 'Other Rites', and would be too prominent if printed after Mattins and Evensong.

Book 5. THE ORDINAL (27) consists of three services, which were originally printed as a separate book, and published after the First Prayer Book was issued. These still have a Title-page (or half-page) of their own, in which they are described with definiteness and solemnity as '*The Form and Manner of Making, Ordaining, and Consecrating of Bishops, Priests, and Deacons according to the Order of the Church of England*'.

THE ANGLICAN PRAYER BOOKS

The wonderful extension of the Anglican Church in recent times is still but little realized. A vast Anglican Communion has been quietly spreading all over the world and is steadily knitting up bonds of fellowship with all the other Churches (outside the isolated Roman Communion) in every country. At the Lambeth Conference of 1930 eighteen Churches or Provinces and two Regional Churches were represented by the 308 bishops who assembled. Here is the official list of the Churches and Provinces within the Anglican Church, those having an English Prayer Book of their own being marked with an asterisk, other special cases with an obelus:

*The Church of England.
 The Church in Wales.
*The Church of Ireland.
*The Episcopal Church in Scotland.
*The Protestant Episcopal Church in the United States of
    America.
 The Province of India, Burma, and Ceylon.
†The Province of South Africa (see p. 145).
*The Church of England in the Dominion of Canada.
 The Province of the West Indies.
 The Church of Australasia.
 The Church of New Zealand and Melanesia.
†The Church in China (Chung Hua Sheng Kung Hui).
†The Church in Japan (Nippon Sei Kokwai).
 Missionary Bishoprics of Asia.
 Missionary Bishoprics of Africa.
 Colonial Dioceses and Missionary Bishoprics in Europe.

These Churches, like the Greek, Russian, and other Orthodox Churches of the East, together form one Communion; but, like the Eastern Churches, they are self-governing, and each has the inherent power to make its own Prayer Book, though the

4. INTERIOR OF CHURCH AT HUBLI
BOMBAY, INDIA
Built by members of criminal tribes now working in the Industrial
Settlement at Hubli.

position of some has not yet been fully regularized in a legal sense. At present, the Churches, Provinces, and Dioceses not marked with an asterisk use the English Prayer Book of 1662, with many permitted additions and deviations. The history of the other Books is given in Chapter XII. The Churches of our Communion in China and Japan have Prayer Books in their own languages, based partly on the English and partly on the American Book.

Thus there is in the world a family of Anglican Service Books, besides the old translations of the English Prayer Book in Latin, French, Welsh, Gaelic (1551–1608), and the later translations in many other languages, such as Tamil, Kafir, Yoruba, Amharic, Cree, Mohawk, Canarese, and Zimshi! In the Russian and other Slav Churches, also, other languages are used besides the Old Slavonic of the normal Russian Service books.

The Church, as we can see from the account of Pentecost in Acts 2: 9, spread at the beginning outside the Roman Empire to the 'Parthians, Medes, Elamites', and others, and recent discoveries have shown how strong the Church was in Mesopotamia, Persia, and Armenia. There were thus for many centuries three great Churches, of which two (the Byzantine and Latin) were in the Roman Empire (the Mediterranean world), while one centred in the Persian Empire and extended to China and India. Thus:

1. ASIAN	2. BYZANTINE	3. LATIN
(Persia, &c.)	(Mediterranean)	

The Asian Church was once very large, but was devastated by the Muslim invaders. It was still numerous and widespread in the 8th and 9th centuries; but in modern times only a few persecuted churches survived. To-day, thanks to the missionaries, the Church in Asia already numbers many millions.

There are four great liturgical families in Christendom, and some minor families, which may be arranged as follows:

THE LITURGICAL FAMILIES

I. ASIAN

1. PERSIAN (miscalled 'East Syrian'): Liturgies of St. Adaeus and St. Maris, and two others. The titles of three more are preserved, and more may be discovered. 2. INDIAN: The Liturgy of the Christians of *St. Thomas in Malabar* belongs to this group.

II. BYZANTINE

SYRIAN (called also 'West Syrian'), the Patriarchate of Antioch, i.e. Syria and Palestine: Syriac Liturgy of St. James, and sixty-four others, most of which are still extant. This is a very ancient rite, being already visible in some detail in the *Catecheses* of St. Cyril of Jerusalem (A.D. 347), in the *Pilgrimage of Etheria* (*c.* 380), and in the writings of St. Chrysostom (347–407), as well as in the so-called *Apostolic Constitutions* of the 4th century.

The *Armenian Liturgy* of St. Athanasius belongs to the Byzantine group. There was a national Church of Armenia before the time of Constantine, when the Roman Empire was still pagan. Once there were ten other liturgies of this greatly persecuted Church.

GREEK: This group is now represented by (*a*) the GREEK Liturgies of St. Chrysostom, St. Basil, and St. Gregory Dialogos, (*b*) the SLAVONIC, as well as Arabic, Chinese, Japanese, Tatar, and other translations of these, used by the Russian and other Slav Churches.

There is also an AFRICAN Group. Egypt: *Coptic Liturgy* of St. Mark, and several others. Abyssinia: *Ethiopic Liturgy* of the Apostles belongs to the same group.

III. LATIN

A. GALLICAN GROUP. 1. *Gallican Liturgy*. The national liturgy of France until the 9th century, when Charlemagne suppressed it, substituting the Roman rite. This liturgy was lost until three Gallican Sacramentaries were discovered and published in 1680 under the names of *Missale Gothicum*, *Missale Gallicum*, and *Missale Francorum*. 2. *Celtic* is a good name for the rites used in Britain before the Anglo-Saxon conquest, and in Scotland and Ireland, together with Wales and Cornwall for centuries after. A good deal has been discovered in recent years by the study of liturgical remains in the Scottish Book of Deer, the Irish Books of Dimma and Mulling, the Stowe Missal, &c., which show that the liturgies of the Celtic Churches were Gallican in character. 3. The *Mozarabic Liturgy* was the national liturgy of Spain till the end of the 11th century, when the Roman rite was forced upon the country. It is now used (with some Roman modifications) in some churches at Toledo and in one chapel at Salamanca. 4. *Ambrosian Liturgy*. Charlemagne's attempt to destroy this in favour of the Roman rite failed; and it is still used in the province of Milan.

B. ROMAN GROUP. 1. *Medieval Rites*. The different parts of west Europe had their own variants of the Roman books, after these had replaced the earlier rites between the 7th and 11th centuries; and there were many local and diocesan uses incorporating some survivals from Gallican customs. 2. *Monastic Rites*. Benedictine, Cistercian, Carthusian, Dominican, now modified, but still in use. 3. The *Roman Missal*, &c., of the present day. The chief peculiarities of the Roman Group are: (*a*) The position of the Great Intercession in the Canon, divided before and after the so-called Words of Institution. (*b*) The absence of the Epiklesis. (*c*) The position of the Pax or Kiss of Peace at a late part of the service.

IV. ANGLICAN

The ANGLICAN GROUP now includes: 1. The *English* Prayer Book; 2. the *American*; 3. the *Scottish*; 4. the *Irish*; 5. the *Canadian*; to which may be added, besides the various translations, the *Chinese* and *Japanese*, which have both English and American features, and the experiments in South Africa and South India.

All these diverse groups, except the Gallican and Celtic sections and the Medieval, which were destroyed by the chauvinism of the Roman see, are in greater or less use to-day; but the Asian section (I) now covers a comparatively small number of people; and the great majority of Asiatics, converted by missionary agencies, at present use the rites of the European and American Churches with which they are severally associated. These Christians of Asia now number many millions, as we have said; and they are increasing at a far more rapid rate than ever happened during the long-drawn conversion of Europe.

CHAPTER IV

THE DEVELOPMENT OF SERVICE BOOKS

IT will be convenient to trace the earlier history of our Church services when we come to deal with them separately, in the third part of this book; in this chapter, therefore, and those which immediately follow, we shall confine ourselves to the history of the Prayer Book itself as one whole book.

Services were in the Primitive Church unfixed in character, as we have seen, and largely extempory. When the words became fixed, the services gradually came to be written out in separate manuscripts. None of the very earliest books (so far as we yet know) have survived. If there were any outlines or handbooks in the 3rd century they may have been destroyed in the last persecution of the Christians by the Emperor Diocletian (303) which included a systematic destruction of Christian literature. Much in the Asian Church was destroyed later by the Muslims. A vast amount of manuscripts all over Europe must have been burnt by the Barbarians, who mastered every country outside the Greek Empire in the Dark Ages, and by the members of the Fourth Crusade who burnt and sacked Constantinople itself. Moreover, the systematic forgeries by the monks of the Dark and Middle Ages must have been accompanied by a much larger amount of destruction of unwelcome evidence about the Early Church; for it is much easier to destroy than to forge.

However, an early book by Sarapion, Bishop of Thmuis, in Egypt (p. 198), of about the year 350, was discovered at Mount Athos in 1894, and it is quite possible that scholars may discover something yet earlier.

It is probable that there were some fixed formulas in the

earliest services, and sentences which look like quotations of these exist in the *Epistle of St. Clement* (*c.* A.D. 96), and a definite form in the *Didaché* of the same early date (see p. 183). A baptismal creed is given in Acts 8: 37, 'I believe that Jesus Christ is the Son of God': but it is only in some of the texts, and may belong to the 2nd century. It is possible that some verses from St. Paul are budding liturgical phrases, e.g. 'Wherefore [it] saith, Awake, thou that sleepest, and arise from the dead, and Christ shall give thee light' (Eph. 5: 14). This seems to be a quotation from some very early Christian hymn. Again, to quote a verse which is very likely later than St. Paul: 'He who was manifested in the flesh, justified in the Spirit, seen of angels, preached unto the Gentiles, believed on in the world, received up into glory' (1 Tim. 3: 16), which latter may have been part of a prayer that the writer was in the habit of using, just as 'The grace of our Lord', in 2 Cor. 13: 14, was perhaps a form of blessing which St. Paul used on general occasions.

There seem to be fragments of local Christian ejaculations or hymns scattered over the Apocalypse, and perhaps in other parts of the New Testament. The reader may find it interesting to look these out for himself—Rev. 4: 8–11; 5: 9, 10, 12, 13; 7: 12; 11: 17; 12: 10–12; 15: 3–4; 19: 1, 6–7; 2 Tim. 2: 11–13; and, besides Eph. 5: 14, perhaps 1: 3–14, and the prayer in Acts 4: 24–30. There are also the great canticles given us by St. Luke in the first two chapters of his Gospel—*Magnificat*, *Benedictus*, *Gloria in Excelsis*, and *Nunc Dimittis*.

We find, in fact, many elements of Christian worship in the New Testament—(1) *Praise*, as in 1 Cor. 14: 26, and in these canticles and hymns; (2) *Prayer*, as in 1 Cor. 15: 14–16, and of course in many other places; (3) *Lessons*, as the reading of Epistles in 1 Thess. 5: 27 and Col. 4: 16, and doubtless also the reading of 'memoirs' of Christ as well as of books of the Old Testament; (4) *Sermons*, as in Acts 20: 7; 1 Tim. 4: 13;

(5) *Prophecy*, probably resembling the utterances and prayers which break the silence of a Quakers' meeting (or of other 'quiet meetings'), as it is mentioned in 1 Cor. 14: 1, 29; 1 Thess. 5: 20, and in 1 Cor. 11: 4, where we learn that women took part in the praying and prophesying, because St. Paul rebuked some for doing this unveiled. This passage is interesting because it shows that the Apostle's injunction, 'Let your women keep silence in the churches' (1 Cor. 14: 34), did not mean that they were not to take any part in the service, but referred to a habit which had grown up amongst the women, of chattering during service time: the men, it seems from the context, interrupted by babbling with 'tongues', or by all prophesying at once, and then the women increased the confusion by asking questions about what they meant—which is not to be wondered at; (6) *Tongues*, which we see by 1 Cor. 14: 23–39, were already becoming somewhat of a babel, and are unfavourably compared by St. Paul with Prophecy; (7) *Almsgiving*, 1 Cor. 16: 1; 2 Cor. 9: 1–15; (8) *The Agapè* (see p. 182), called by St. Paul a dominical supper, or Lord's supper, *kyriakon deipnon*, in 1 Cor. 11: 20–2; (9) *Unction*, in Jas. 5: 14, with Exorcism (Acts 16: 18) and the manifold ministry of healing; and (10) the great religious acts of *Baptism* and the *Laying on of Hands*, which we shall recur to in Chapters XVI and XVIII.

After the Apostolic Age we find some allusions to be mentioned in Chapter XV; but the earliest real service book we have is that of Sarapion (*c.* 350). This precious document is a 'Sacramentary'—that is to say, it contains the celebrant's prayers in the Communion Service (p. 198) and other rites. The so-called Canons of Hippolytus must be placed later than Sarapion; because, although Hippolytus himself lived in the 3rd century, the Canons that bear his name are full of interpolations of the 4th century and probably also of the 5th and even of the 6th century, as Dom Connolly shows in his *The*

So-called Egyptian Church Order (Cambridge Texts and Studies). Since early evidence is still so scarce, the greatest care is needed in studying it.

We have to pass over another century or more before we find any extant books as complete as Sarapion's; though we know from other writings that such books did exist. From the 7th century onwards the history of service books can be traced with ever-increasing clearness. They consisted of three groups, the *Divine Service*, the *Sacraments*, and the *Occasional Services*, these latter including all the services used upon occasions such as Marriage, Ordination, and the Reconciliation of Penitents.

5. A GOSPEL BOOK
The four Gospels, 9th century, are bound in a silver cover of the 14th.

The scribes, however, did not consider so much the grouping of the services as the people who would have to use the books. In those days, when the penning of manuscripts at great labour and expense was the only way of making a service book, the scribe naturally would not insert any matter that was not necessary to the minister for whom the book was written. Thus the bishop or priest had his Sacramentary, consisting of the celebrant's part of the Eucharist, but containing also his part for other services, such as Baptism, Marriage, or Ordination. The majority of our Prayer Book collects are expanded from three Old Roman Sacramentaries—the Leonine (6th century), the Gelasian (early 8th century), and the Gregorian (c. 800). The deacon also had his own Gospel Book for the part it was his duty to read, the subdeacon had his Epistle Book or Lectionary, and the singers had musical choir books and Psalters for their use.

We have a list of the manuscripts required in England at the close of the Anglo-Saxon period in Archbishop Ælfric's Canons (c. 1006), and for the Norman period in Archbishop Winchelsea's Constitutions (c. 1300): these may be arranged as follows:

DIVINE SERVICE	HOLY COMMUNION	OCCASIONAL SERVICES
	Anglo-Saxon List	
Psalter	Missal	Handbook
Reading book	Gospel Book	———
Passional	Epistle Book	Also Gerime or
Song book		Kalendar
	Norman List	
Psalter	Missal	Ordinal (a directory)
Legend	Gradual	Manual
Antiphoner	Troper	

The Passional consisted of the 'passions' or stories of the martyrdom of the saints. The Legend or Reading book contained the Scriptures, lives of the saints, and homilies, which were to be read as lessons (*legendae*). The Gradual contained the portions of the Psalter sung between the Epistle and the Gospel, and also those sung for the Introit and at other places in the Mass, as it was now called. The Antiphonal or Antiphoner contained the musical parts of the services (originally the Gradual was known as the Antiphonarium Missae). The Troper consisted of interpolations into the chant: these additions to the traditional music became very large, but after the twelfth century little except the Sequences (sung after the Gradual and Alleluya, between the Epistle and Gospel) was left of them. The Manual or Handbook contained the Occasional Services. The bishop's own books are not mentioned here, the 'Ordinal' meaning a directory of services.

From the 13th century till the Reformation the 'use' of Salisbury Cathedral was followed in the greater part of England (excluding Hereford which had a use of its own, and parts of the North which followed the York use), and also throughout the mainland of Scotland and in parts of Ireland and Wales. A full list of the books belonging to this widely-spread use may be arranged thus:

Sarum Books

DIVINE SERVICE	HOLY COMMUNION	OCCASIONAL SERVICES
Psalter	Sacramentary (priest's part)	Pontifical (bishop's services)
Legend	Gospel Book	Manual (priest's)
Antiphonal	Epistle Book	Also Pie or Kalendar
Hymnal	Gradual	Also, towards the end
Collectar	Troper (Sequences)	of the Middle Ages, Processional

As the Middle Ages went on, the Breviary services became overladen and corrupt. Always more suited for monastic use than for that of parish churches, they grew more and more unfit for any but the clergy, and even for the clergy they became very burdensome. Although it was considered seemly for the lay folk before the Reformation, not only to be present at Mass on Sundays, but also at Mattins and Evensong, these services,

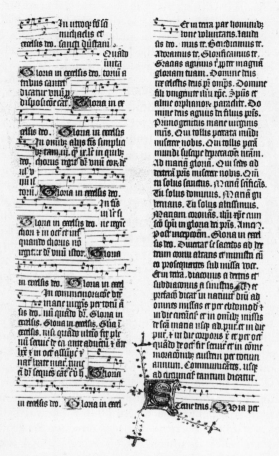

6. PAGE OF AN ILLUMINATED MISSAL

Page of a very fine MS. Sarum Missal, 15th century, with music,
showing the *Gloria in Excelsis* with interpolations, e.g. 'For thou only
art holy, sanctifying Mary'; 'Thou only art the Lord, ruling Mary'.

especially Mattins with its many lessons and elaborate structure, had long ceased to be edifying to the people, who had to be content indeed with their own prayers. They were cut off from the choir offices also by the language being unintelligible: in this, as in many other ways, the Middle Ages were the least Catholic ages of the Church.

7. A LOW MASS
The Priest is served by a lad wearing a rochet.
From a 15th-century MS.

Not only did the choir services become overladen and corrupt, but the increasing cult of the saints and the spread of votive or special services caused a great multiplication of masses, which could not all be rendered with the ceremonial dignity traditional in the Church. The Eucharist in the purer ages of the Church had been a weekly service of fellowship. It now became an isolated daily rite, commonly regarded as a propitiatory sacrifice at which an act of magic was performed, while Communion was an annual duty. Already there had grown up what were called Low Masses and Private Masses—that is to say, masses celebrated by a single priest, with only a clerk or even a boy to help him, and with no communicants. These were not only customary in small churches, where often there was little else; but they multiplied everywhere, and nowhere more than in the great churches in towns, which became filled with side altars and small chapels, where various foundation masses were said, the stipends of which proved a temptation to the clergy to say as many of them as possible.

Both the paucity of ministers in small churches and the multiplication of services in the larger brought it about that it was more convenient to have the different parts of the service combined in one book than to have them separate. Each set was therefore generally made into one book in the later Middle Ages, thus:

DIVINE SERVICE	HOLY COMMUNION	OCCASIONAL SERVICES
Breviary	Missal	Pontifical Manual Processional

Then came the invention of printing in the middle of the 15th century, which largely removed the original reason for having a number of separate books. There began at once to appear printed Missals, Grails, Breviaries, Antiphoners, Pontificals, Manuals, and Processionals.

Now, one of the results of the English Reformation has been partly to restore the old co-operative method of worship—or, as we say, the congregational method, though it is really more than this. The co-operative method not only gives the congregation its part in the service, but also gives their parts to the gospeller, the epistoler, the preacher, the special chanters or clerks, and the choir, as well as the priest; and thus makes the service a great united act of worship.

This restoration was not possible till the Reformers set about to render the old Latin services in the mother tongue of the people. Their work was made much easier by the invention of printing, which not only created a desire for reform by spreading knowledge, but also made it at last possible for those who could read English to follow the services in their own books.

Printing, then, helped the Reformers; but their work would

not have been possible at all in England had it not been for another cause. There was now a language which every one spoke.

The former use of Latin had not been merely due to an irrational conservatism—though people are always apt to be irrationally conservative about their prayers and hymns. There were better reasons: Latin was the universal language of educated people in western Europe, and thus there had been much convenience in using it in the former ages when there was no other literary language. In England, for instance, for centuries after the Conquest, French had been the language of the aristocracy and of the law courts (of which we still have traces in such phrases as 'Le roi le veult', 'Oyez, Oyez'); the common people spoke various English dialects which were almost like different languages, so that a book written in London would have been unintelligible to a Yorkshireman; and therefore it is no wonder that learned people wrote in Latin, which was for them a kind of Esperanto amid the babel of tongues. In the 14th century, however, there came to be a real English language, and Wyclif (†1384) and Chaucer (†1400) were able to produce the first books in the noble library of modern English literature, the former being especially famous for the translation of the Bible—by himself and John Purvey, who was the editor, Wyclif translating the Gospels, and probably the whole New Testament, and possibly part of the Old.

It was therefore possible at the beginning of the 16th century not only to print the services, but to print them in an English which Englishmen all over the country could understand. Before the middle of that century the Bible had been printed in English, and thus became universally accessible and intelligible; and just before the middle year—in 1549—the First English Prayer Book was printed. It now became possible to restore fuller extracts from the Bible in Divine Service; for

8. ILLUMINATED FRONTISPIECE TO THE FAMOUS COPY OF THE GREAT BIBLE AT ST. JOHN'S COLLEGE, CAMBRIDGE

King Henry VIII is distributing Bibles to bishops (on the left, in rochet and tippet), and to courtiers (on the right). Below are a bishop (as above, but with mitre), a preacher in surplice, almuce, and square cap, a doctor, and lay folk of all classes.

the whole Bible—now a comparatively cheap book—could be used side by side with the Prayer Book; and these two volumes would supply every one's need.

Formerly the lay folk had only been able to follow the services in little simplified books of their own, and even these were an expensive luxury; but now every one could follow the services word for word, and those who knew their letters could read them in their own books. So the old books that we have described were further condensed into two, the *Bible* and the *Prayer Book*.

Now, if the reader will turn to the second Preface in the English Prayer Book, called '*Concerning the Service of the Church*', he will find the reasons for the liturgical Reformation set forth in admirable terms, though indeed this preface is concerned with the Divine Service, that is, with Mattins and Evensong only. The main reasons given are six:

1. Great stress is laid on the need of reading the Bible as a whole in Divine Service each year.

2. Abuses must be got rid of. The 'uncertain Stories, and Legends', and 'vain Repetitions' had crowded out the Bible-reading which had been the 'godly and decent order of the ancient Fathers', so that, after three or four chapters of a book had been read out, all the rest were left unread.

3. The language spoken to the people in the church must be such 'as they might understand, and have profit by hearing the same', as St. Paul had urged.

4. The Psalms must be said regularly, as the ancient Fathers had said them; instead of a few being 'daily said, and the rest utterly omitted'.

5. 'The number and hardness of the Rules called the *Pie*' must be amended. This Pie was a perpetual kalendar, showing what things should be said at all possible services and combination of services. If a parson did not give considerable study

Eigitur clementiss. ime pater : per iesum christū filium tuum dūm nostrū : supplices rogamus corpo re u, clinato d ōnec dicat. ac pet. m̄ Dic erigens se sacerdos osculetur altare a dextris sacrificii dices. uti accepta habeas et benedicas. Dic faciat sacerdos tres cruces : super calicem et panem dicendo. Hec ✠ dona. hec ✠ munera. hec ✠ sancta sacrificia illibata. Factis signaculis super calicem eleuet manus suas ita dicens.

IN primis que tibi off. rimus p ecclesia tua sancta catholica : quā pacificare : custodire : adunare : et regere digneris toto orbe terrarū vna cū famulo tuo ~~papa~~ nostro ᷓᷓ̄. et antistite nostro. N. id est p̄pio episcopo tanta ✠ ~~rege no~~ ~~stro~~ N. et dicūtur noiatim. Sequatur et omnibus orthodoxis : atq̃ catholice et apostolice fidei cultoribus. Dic oret pro viuis.

MEmento dn̄e famulorūz famularūq̃ tuarū. N. et. N. In qua oratione ordo debet atten di propter ordinē caritatis. Quum quis orat sacerdos. Primo pro se ipso. Secūdo p patre et matre carnali et spūali et p alus parentibus Tertio p amicis specialibus paro chianis et alus. Quarto pro oibus astantibus. Quinto p omni pp̄lo xp̄iano. Et potest hic sacerdos des ilios amicos deo cōmēdare. Cōsu lo tam̄ vt nullius ibidē nomina mo retur : tū ppter cordis distracti one tū ppter imultitudines q̃ po. sunt tū per agelos maios : tū propter

alia pericula. Et olim ecclesiasticis quorū tibi fides cognita et nota deuotio. p q̄bus tibi offerimus vel q̄ tibi offerūt hoc sacrificiū laudis pro se suisq̃ oibus : pro redēptione animarū suarum : p spe salutis et incolumitatis sue : tibiq̃ reddunt vota sua eterno deo viuo et vero.

COmmunicātes et memoriā venerātes. In primis glouose semper virginis Inclinado pa rūper dicat. marie genitricis dei et dn̄i nostri iesu xp̄i. Sed et beatorū apostolorū ac martyrū tuorū Petri Pauli. Andree. Jacobi Joannis Thome Jacobi Philippi Bartholomei Mathei Symōis ✠ Thadei Lini Cleti Clemētis Sixti Corne lii Cypriani Laurentii Crisogoni Joannis et pauli Cosme et Damiani. Et oim sanctorū tuorū quorū meritis precibusq̃ cōcedas : vt in oibus protectiōis tue muniamur auxilio. Per eūdē xp̄m dn̄m nostrū. Amē. Dic respiciat sacerdos hostiā cū magna veneratione dicens.

HAnc igitur oblationē servitutis nostre : sed et cūcte fami lie tue q̃s dn̄e vt placatus accipias diesq̃ n̄ros in tua pace disponas : atq̃ ab eterna dānatiōe nos eripi : et in electorū tuorū : iubeas grege numerari. Per xp̄m dn̄m nr̄z. Amē hic iterum respiciat hostiam dices.

QUam oblationē tu deus oi potens in omnibus q̄sumus. Dic faciat tres cruces super vtrūq̃ cum dicat Bene ✠ dictam asc̄ri ✠ ptam:ra ✠ am:rationabi lem:acceptabilemq̃ facere digneris vt nobis. Dic faciat cruce super pa nem dicens. cor ✠ pus. Dic super ✠p. liu.

9. THE BEGINNING OF THE CANON, FROM A PRINTED SARUM MISSAL OF 1520

The word *papa* (pope) has been erased in the reign of Henry VIII, and written in again in that of Queen Mary, when also 'rege nostro' two lines below, has been altered.

to these intricacies before he began the service, he could hardly help going wrong: indeed, as the Preface says, 'many times there was more business to find out what should be read, than to read it when it was found out'.

6. There had been great diversity of uses. The Preface mentions the uses of Salisbury, Hereford, Bangor, York, and Lincoln; and declares that 'now from henceforth all the whole Realm shall have but one Use'. The uses of Bangor and Lincoln seem to have been like that of Exeter, little more than variants of Sarum. London also had its own use till 1414, when the Dean and Chapter of St. Paul's adopted the Sarum Use, retaining their own ceremonial.

Thus the time was ripe. The English Bible was in people's hands; many were dissatisfied with the old services both because they had become complicated and burdensome (see p. 160) and because they contained things which are now admitted to have been superstitious, childish, and untrue. In the reign of Henry VIII (1533) the Bishops in Convocation proclaimed the freedom of the English Church, by declaring that no foreign bishop (such as the Pope) could have authority over it; and thus the English Church was placed on the same level of autonomy as the Orthodox Churches of the East. In the reign of Edward VI (1549) the first English Prayer Book was published.

The Reformation had come. Its liturgical result in our present Book may be tabulated as on p. 37.

Here, then, is the liturgical explanation of our taking the Bible and the Prayer Book to Church. But it will occur at once to the reader that on Sundays we take a hymn book as well; and as a matter of fact hymn books have been bound up with the Prayer Book from the 16th century onwards. The modern hymn book occupies indeed an important part in our more popular services, and contains a great many more hymns than the old Latin hymnals.

DIVINE SERVICE	HOLY COMMUNION	OCCASIONAL SERVICES
	Books of the Middle Ages	
Psalter	Sacramentary	Pontifical
Legend	Gospel Book	Manual
Antiphonal	Epistle Book	Processional
Hymnal	Gradual	Pie
Collectar	Troper	
	Combined Books of the Middle Ages	
Breviary	Missal	

Books of the English Reformation

The Prayer Book
The Bible

DIVINE SERVICE	HOLY COMMUNION	OCCASIONAL SERVICES
Morning Prayer	The Collects, Epistles, and Gospels	The Orders of Baptism
Evening Prayer		The Catechism
Creed of St. Athanasius	The Order of Holy Communion	Confirmation
Prayers and Thanksgivings		Matrimony
The Psalter		Visitation and Communion of the Sick
The Bible		Burial of the Dead
		Churching of Women
(The Litany is the equivalent of the Processional; the Order of the Psalter, Kalendar, Tables, &c., supplies the place of the Pie.)		Commination
		The Ordinal

There is also a floating collection of additional services, the most important being the Form for the Consecration of Churches and in England the Coronation Service; while the Accession Service is by authority printed with the English Prayer Book. Three other State Services were added in the Reign of Charles II, and were excluded in that of Victoria; and a form 'At the Healing' (for use when the King laid his hands on sick persons, 'touching for the King's Evil') was sometimes printed with the Prayer Book in the 17th century and in the reign of Queen Anne.

While we are discussing the way in which the old Latin services were transformed into the Prayer Book, it may be worth while for the benefit of our brethren of the Eastern and Roman Catholic Churches to show how it is that, in addition to Confirmation, Orders, and Matrimony, two of the ancient Occasional Services, the so-called lesser sacraments of Penance and Unction, have still a place in the Anglican Church, though they do not appear among the twenty-seven Contents which are given above. But we ought to say frankly that they are very little used by the English-speaking peoples—as indeed they have lost their former hold also in such countries as France and Spain, and those of eastern Europe.

The Visitation of the Sick contains express directions for confession and absolution, and thus this service includes the former of these rites; nor are individual confession and absolution confined to the sick, for they are offered also to the whole in the First Exhortation of the Communion Service, though they are wisely left as a voluntary matter for those in distress of conscience; while general and public confession and absolution are used at Divine Service and at every celebration of the Liturgy. The Medieval reckoning of seven, Sacraments—for it is not earlier—includes Unction also. Now a service for Anointing the Sick appeared in the First Prayer Book, but was omitted in the second and in all subsequent revisions, the reason being that Unction had become in practice a service for the dying instead of a sacrament of health. The Lambeth Conference of 1908 decided not to recommend the Unction of the Sick, but to allow its use, expressing a hope that the other apostolic act for helping the sick, the Laying on of Hands, might

10. THE ANOINTING OF HER MAJESTY QUEEN ALEXANDRA

By the Archbishop of York. The other prelates are (from left to right) the Bishop of Winchester, the Archbishop of Canterbury, the Bishop of Norwich, the Bishop of Oxford

By special permission of Messrs. Thos. Agnew & Sons, the owners of the copyright of Professor Tuxen's picture.

be used with prayers for the restoration of health. Those who are inclined to press the importance of Unction should remember that in the New Testament, and for long afterwards, the Laying on of Hands was used at least as much as anointing for helping the sick. It is therefore rightly to be regarded as an alternative and perhaps a better form; just as we administer Confirmation by the Laying on of Hands, whereas in the Eastern Church, and in most of the West, Confirmation is administered by anointing. In the last American Revision both forms are included in the service for the Visitation of the Sick.

The floating mass of additional services is indeed a very important factor in Anglican religion, and we should form a wrong estimate of Anglicanism if we ignored it. The influence of Hymn books alone upon worship and religion is enormous; *Hymns Ancient and Modern*, the *Hymnal Companion*, *Church Hymns*, and in the 20th century, the American *Hymnal*, the Canadian *Book of Common Praise*, the *English Hymnal*, and *Songs of Praise*, have proved a valuable means of allowing each generation to enrich our services; modern hymnals keep us in touch with the thought and feeling of our own age, besides having the happy result of enabling Christians of other communions to contribute to our service, and we to theirs. Closely allied to hymns are the modern anthems, which in cathedral and collegiate churches are collected in Anthem books, thus adding a fourth to the volumes required for Divine Service each day. Hymns, carols, and anthems place every form of sacred vocal music at the service of the Church. Nor are they unauthorized additions: the existence of these collections of hymns and anthems which provide Anglicanism with so precious an element of freedom has been sanctioned by authority ever since the 16th century: four hymns at one service were authorized in 1566 (see p. 84); and hymns have legal and canonical authority under the Shortened Services Act of 1872 (see p. 129), and the latter are mentioned in the twice repeated rubric, 'In Quires and Places where they sing, here followeth the Anthem'. Further evidence about this is given in *Songs of Praise Discussed* (1933).

Another notable and ancient feature, which also has the invaluable quality of adaptability to varying needs, is the Bidding Prayer in the pulpit, which is not mentioned in the English Prayer Book, though it is now printed in the American, Scottish, and Canadian Books; but it is ordered by the 55th Canon (1603) to be used before all Sermons, Lectures, and Homilies, and has formed part of the Sunday Eucharist from Anglo-Saxon times onwards.

There are also other additional forms of service at the present day, authorized in different Churches or dioceses in great number—many in book form. When the English Church settled down in the reign of Elizabeth, no less than forty-four forms of public prayer, fasting, thanksgiving, for all sorts of occasions— plague, war, political crises, &c.—were issued between 1560 and 1600; besides the Latin Commemoration of Benefactors (which is still used in Westminster Abbey and elsewhere) and the Collect, Epistle, and Gospel for Funerals, in the Latin Prayer Book of 1560. These have been reprinted by the Parker Society in *Liturgical Services, Queen Elizabeth*. The same Society printed a volume of *Private Prayers, put forth by authority*, between 1559 and 1578, the private devotions in this collection including the Primer, which contains among other things forms for Lauds and Prime, Terce, Sext, and None, with office hymns and antiphons, and the Dirge for the departed, with prayers for them.

It may be interesting here to mention some of the forms of prayer and thanksgiving issued by authority after 1600, copies of which are preserved in the Library of the British Museum: 1626 (Thirty Years War); 1665 (Victory over the Dutch); 1666 (After the Fire of London), which did not go entirely out of use till 1860; 1784 (End of the War of American Independence); 1789 (Recovery of George III); 1798 (Battle of the Nile); 1815 (Battle of Waterloo); 1847 (Irish Famine); 1856 (Several forms of thanksgiving during the Crimean War); 1859 (End of the Indian Mutiny); 1866 (During the Prevalence of the Cholera); 1887 and 1897 (Queen Victoria's two Jubilees). Many memorial services, forms for use in time of war, and during elections of representatives, and for other public occasions, have been issued by authority during the last half-century. And in America there is a special Book of Offices as well.

11. TITLE-PAGE OF BISHOP ANDREWES'S FORM FOR THE CONSECRATION OF A CHURCH
Engraved by Hollar.

There have been also many local services, such as that at Windsor on St. George's Day, with its great procession, a picture of which we give on p. 175, and the picturesque annual distribution of the Royal Maundy in Westminster Abbey. The Bishops have also had to make their own pontificals, since the Prayer Book only contains four services for their special use. Thus we have forms for the ordination of Deaconesses, the admission of readers, the profession of sisters, and many dedications and benedictions, including forms for the consecration of churches, chapels, and churchyards. Bishop Andrewes drew up a form of Consecration of a Church in 1620, Convocation in 1712 and 1715. There are similar forms in the American Prayer Book and other books, as we have already mentioned, and one in England by Bishop John Wordsworth (1898), among others.

So far indeed from the Anglican Church being poverty-stricken in liturgical matter, it suffers rather from a plethora of additional services. A selection of those in common use to-day, so far as the Eucharist is concerned, was made by Bishops W. H. Frere and S. M. Taylor, and the present writer, and in 1903 published in an altar book called *The English Liturgy* (Rivingtons)—and in a small form in *The Sanctuary*, wherein half the additional Collects, Epistles, and Gospels had been already authorized. This is used extensively as an altar Book. The Deposited Book—the English Revision of 1927–8—failed to secure the final authority of the Convocations and the Crown, and is therefore without authority. Its use, however, in providing informal guidance for many deviations of the present day is considerable. The bishop of a diocese has not the power to authorize this Deposited Book; but most bishops have let it be understood that they will not take action against those who confine their deviations from the Prayer Book to those suggested in 1928. The history of the more successful revisions in America, Scotland, Ireland, and Canada is given in Chapter XIV.

Thus are the needs of each generation brought within the scope of our common intercession and devotion. We are not confined within the corners of the Prayer Book; nor is the ancient tree dead which has borne such abundant fruit during the Christian era.

PART II
THE STAGES OF LITURGICAL REFORM

CHAPTER V

THE FIRST STAGES OF LITURGICAL CHANGE

WE explained in the last chapter how at the Reformation the old Latin services were translated into English, shortened, simplified, altered, and printed in one volume, *The Book of Common Prayer*, which with the English Bible forms the liturgical basis of our worship; though these two books are supplemented in all the Churches of the Anglican communion by hymns, anthems, the bidding of prayer, and additional prayers and services.

But this process of Reformation did not happen all at once: it took more than a century, beginning in the reign of Henry VIII (1544) and ending in that of Charles II (1662) during which five English Prayer Books were produced, the fifth being the one which is still used in England, while the Anglican Churches of America, Scotland, Canada, and Ireland have produced books of their own, with many useful variations.

All this is of course not an innovation of the Reformation period. There have always been many different liturgies and classes of books in Christendom: the Eastern Church uses many languages; even in the Churches of the modern Papacy, where every effort has been made for the predominance of the Roman rite, several other rites in different languages are allowed in certain specified places.

Thus there was abundant precedent both for reforming and for translating the service books; nor is it likely that the process will ever stop—indeed, in 1911, the Roman Church entirely rearranged the Psalter in what might be called a revolutionary manner, were it not that learned scholars of the Latin West had been urging some such reform for nearly four hundred years. This of course meant a new and reformed Roman Breviary.

Now in the 16th century the air was full of reforming projects; and two foreign books had considerable effect upon Archbishop Cranmer and the other English Reformers—the

12. READING A CHAINED BIBLE IN ST. PAUL'S CATHEDRAL, LONDON
From a 19th-century picture, inaccurate in some details, by Harvey.

Reformed Roman *Breviary* of Cardinal Quiñones, and the *Consultation* of Hermann, Archbishop of Cologne—indeed our second Preface, 'Concerning the Service of the Church', is a restatement by Cranmer of Quiñones's arguments for the reform of the Breviary.

HISTORY OF THE CHANGES

The reform of our services began with the introduction of the English Bible of 1535, fourteen years before the year when the first English Prayer Book appeared. The Bible was in 1536 ordered to be set up in every church, so that it might be read aloud out of service time; and eight years later, Convocation ordered that a chapter of the Bible should be read in English at Mattins after the *Te Deum* and at Evensong after the *Magnificat*. Thus the Lectern may remind us of the first stage in reform. The Litany-desk tells of the second stage; for, though the Litany was not sung kneeling till three years after, that beautiful service itself was produced by the genius of Cranmer, and ordered to be used in 1544.

Then followed the introduction into the Latin services of certain other English features which are mentioned in the summary below:

THE FIRST STAGES

1534 (*Henry VIII*). Convocation petitions the King for an authorized English Version of the Bible.

1535. Coverdale's Bible.

1536. The Bible ordered to be set up in every church.
New edition of the Sarum Breviary, in Latin, but with the name of the Roman Pontiff and other things omitted.

1543. **Lessons in English.** A chapter of the Bible to be read after *Te Deum* and *Magnificat*.

1544. **The English Litany.**

1544–7. Experiments. The *Rationale*, or explanation of the Ceremonies to be used in the Church of England. First and Second Drafts of reformed services in Latin. Cranmer defers translating the Processional.

1547 (*Edward VI*). AUGUST. Beginning of more radical changes by means of the Injunctions (without the authority of Convocation or Parliament): Book of Homilies to be read; At High Mass, Epistle and Gospel to be read in English; New form of Bidding Prayer; and some changes in Breviary services.

NOVEMBER. Convocation meets (at the opening Mass, *Gloria in Excelsis*, Creed, and *Agnus* sung in English), and approves Communion in both kinds.

1548. JANUARY and FEBRUARY. The Council (without the authority of

Convocation or Parliament) forbids the special ancient ceremonies of Candlemas, Ash Wednesday, Palm Sunday, and Good Friday; and the use of the Blessed Bread and Holy Water.

MARCH. **The Order of the Communion,** drawn up by sundry 'grave and well-learned prelates', provides for Communion in both kinds, and is to come into use at Easter by Royal proclamation. This Order consists of the following, inserted before the Communion in the Latin Service: First Exhortation, Second Exhortation, 'Ye that do truly', the Confession, the Absolution and Comfortable Words, 'We do not presume', the Words of Administration in both kinds (first part), 'The Peace of God' (without the Blessing), a Note that the bread is to be as heretofore (round wafers) and each wafer is to be broken for Communion, and a Note that if the Chalice is exhausted the priest is to consecrate afresh, beginning *Simili modo postquam coenatum est*, 'Likewise after Supper', 'without any levation or lifting up'.

APRIL and SEPTEMBER. Preaching forbidden, owing to the opposition in many parishes.

MAY. St. Paul's and other churches 'sung all the service in English, both Mattins, Mass, and Evensong': it therefore appears that these services of the First Prayer Book were already drafted, at least in some experimental form, the choir services being reduced to two, Mattins and Evensong.

At the accession of the boy-king, it is clear that the whole atmosphere was changed: the power passed into the hands of the knot of men who ruled in King Edward's name. Archbishop Cranmer stands apart, leading the bishops, restraining the extremists, and yet himself moving farther along the lines of reform. He was no Luther to cry in the face of the world, 'Here stand I: I can do no other'; but he was able to bring his own great gift to the Reformation—a power of liturgical art which places him among the great prose-writers of the world. Others worked with him and after him, as others had worked before; and the beauty of their united product is a witness to the greatness of that age of literature which covered the hundred years between the First Prayer Book and the last, and gave us the writings of Shakespeare, Bacon, and Milton, as well as five English Prayer Books and the Authorized Version of the

13. KING EDWARD VI RECEIVING THE BIBLE FROM CERTAIN BISHOPS

Behind them are two priests in gown or surplice and tippet, on the right is a group of peers.

From Cranmer's *Catechismus,* 1548.

Bible. But side by side with the constructive work of the bishops, there went the destructive work of the Protector and his allies, carried out unconstitutionally by proclamations and injunctions.

During the second year of Edward VI the divines were

14. ARCHBISHOP CRANMER

From the painting by Flicius, 1546, in the National Portrait Gallery.

He is in his outdoor habit of cassock, rochet, chimere, tippet of sables, and square cap.

engaged upon their task; and, as we have seen, the new English services were tried at St. Paul's and other places. At the close of that regnal year (in January, 1549), the First Prayer Book became law by the First Act of Uniformity, and by March, 1549, the book was published. Whether it had the formal consent of Convocation, as well as that of the two Houses of Parliament (all the members of which were of course communicant Churchmen), we do not know for certain; but the bishops voted for it, by a majority of ten to eight, in the House of Lords, and two letters of the king state that it received also the assent of the other clergy in their synods and convocations. The names of the divines who compiled the First Prayer Book are also hidden in some obscurity; but we know that they represented both the reforming and the conservative side, and it is nearly certain that among them were Bishops Ridley, Holbeach, Thirlby, and Goodrich, as well as Archbishop Cranmer.

15. BISHOP RIDLEY
From a later print.

Let us here take up again our table of events. Cranmer had doubtless been working at the translation of the Latin services for some years: we can imagine with what joy he had turned from the racking cares of State to the quiet solace of that literary work for which God had designed him. One would suppose that the main part of the English Prayer Book was ready a year or two before it was issued: he could not well have rested after the production, four years earlier, of the great English Litany; he must have felt his powers, and rejoiced in them. One pictures him with the manuscript ready, waiting his opportunity to put it forth; then, on King Henry's death, calling committee-meetings of the sundry 'grave and well-learned prelates', sending the Order of the Communion to the

16. BISHOP GOODRICH
From his brass in Ely Cathedral.
He was the author of the Two Duties in
the Catechism.

printers, and (in March, 1548) issuing this second instalment of the Prayer Book; then he must have had copies made of 'Mattins, Mass, and Evensong', so that two months later these services could be sung in English at St. Paul's, and a few days after at Westminster Abbey. With the experience thus gained, his fellow-divines would have helped Cranmer to put finishing-touches on the work, testing it in the Royal Chapel between May and September, and working also at the rest of the Prayer Book; and we know that in September a further step was taken by an order to the college-chapels of Cambridge to conform in 'Mass, Mattins, and Evensong, and all divine service' to the use of the King's Chapel. Three months later the bishops are discussing the new book in the House of Lords.

SUMMARY OF EVENTS

1548. MAY. English Services at St. Paul's and Westminster.

SEPTEMBER. English Services ordered for Cambridge University.

DECEMBER. Debates in Parliament on the First Prayer Book (and probably in Convocation also).

17. MERBECKE'S BOOK OF COMMON PRAYER NOTED

Facsimile of the two last pages.

First Metrical Psalter (nineteen psalms by *Sternhold*) about now. (The 2nd Edition was in 1549, with thirty-seven psalms.)

1549. JANUARY 21ST. First Act of Uniformity. The First Prayer Book becomes law.

MARCH 7TH. First Prayer Book printed and published.

JUNE 9TH. Date fixed by the Act for the Book to be everywhere used.

JUNE 10TH. Armed rebellions against the Act, especially in the distant West of England. The insurgents demand the old ceremonies—Holy water, Images, Ashes, Palms, &c., and the service in Latin, also the recall of the English Bible because it led to heresy, the Mass without communicants, and Communion only once a year.

1550. *The Book of Common Prayer Noted*, by John Merbecke, published. This is Merbecke's famous musical setting, which is still so much used.

MARCH. **The English Ordinal issued,** containing the Ordering of Deacons, the Ordering of Priests, and the Consecration of Bishops. The essential parts of the old rite were carefully retained, but the ceremonial was much reduced.

1549–51. The Foreign Reformers (Bucer, Peter Martyr, &c.) criticize the First Prayer Book.

1551. Third Edition of the *Old Version* of metrical psalms, seven psalms by *Hopkins* being added to *Sternhold's*.

CHAPTER VI
THE FIRST ENGLISH PRAYER BOOK

THE First Prayer Book was an English simplification, condensation, and reform of the old Latin services, done with care and reverence in a genuine desire to remove the degeneracy of the Medieval rites by a return to antiquity. It has been frequently reprinted in our own time, and can easily be obtained. Here we must content ourselves with a brief summary.

The *Contentes of this Booke* are fourteen in number—Preface ['There was never any thing by the wit of man so well devised' —now our second preface]; Tables and Kalendar; Mattins and Evensong; Introits, Collects, Epistles, and Gospels; Holy Communion; Baptism; Confirmation and Catechism; Matrimony; Visitation and Communion of the Sick [including an Order for Unction]; Burial; Purification of Women; A Declaration of Scripture with certain prayers to be used the first Day of Lent [The Commination]; Of Ceremonies omitted or retained [now our third preface]; Certain Notes.

Mattins and Evensong begin with the Lord's Prayer, and end with the Third Collect: no alternatives are provided to *Benedictus*, *Magnificat*, or *Nunc Dimittis*. Otherwise these services are the same as our present ones; but it is compulsory to use *Benedicite* in the place of *Te Deum* in Lent, and the Athanasian Creed (printed after Evensong) is ordered for use immediately after *Benedictus* six times a year—at Christmas, the Epiphany, Easter, the Ascension, Pentecost, and Trinity Sunday.

The Introits for the Communion consist of whole Psalms. The Collects are mainly those which we still use, but some of our best have been written later, e.g. Advent 3, Easter Even; and some have since been expanded, e.g. St. Stephen and St. John, or altered, e.g. Innocents' Day. Introits, collects, &c., are also given for a second Communion on Christmas and Easter Day, and for St. Mary Magdalene, which were omitted from the Second Book. The American, Irish, and Scottish Books have restored the first two of these; the Canadian has restored only the Christmas collect, 'O God, who makest us glad'. The second collect for Easter in the First Book was also the collect for Easter 1, as it still is in all the books. The Scottish Book has a new collect for Mary Magdalene.

The Liturgy: the First Model

It is in the Communion that the greatest differences from our present English Liturgy appear, though here again the Scottish and American Liturgies have gone back behind the changes of the Second Prayer Book to the model of the First. The title is 'The Supper of the Lorde, and the holy Communion, commonly called the Masse'. The main differences from the present English Services are as follows: Ninefold Kyrie without Decalogue, followed by *Gloria in Excelsis*. Immediately after the Offertory follows the *Sursum Corda*, Preface, and *Sanctus*, followed by the prayer 'for the whole state of Christes churche' (without the words 'militant', &c.); continuing with a commemoration of the saints, 'And here we do geve unto thee moste high praise, and hartie thankes for the wonderfull grace and vertue, declared in all thy sainctes', &c.

Then follows the Prayer of Consecration, which includes an *Epiklesis*, that is an invocation of the Holy Spirit to hallow the gifts of Bread and Wine. This insertion of the Epiklesis (which Cranmer took mainly from the Eastern Liturgy of St. Basil) was an important step. The form appeared in the 4th century (p. 200) and is in the Eastern Liturgies of the present day, where it is regarded as the actual consecration at the Eucharist. The Roman Liturgy, on the other hand, has no definite Epiklesis (p. 215), and Latin theologians have for ages laid the stress on the Words of Institution, so-called (they were really words of administration), 'This is my body . . . This is my blood'. This stress was increased in the Middle Ages by new ceremonies such as the Elevation; and consequently there arose the idea that the Eucharist is consecrated merely by the repetition of our Lord's words. Cranmer probably knew that there was no justification for this idea in early

18. THE ORNAMENTS OF THE FIRST PRAYER BOOK
From a pre-Reformation MS., c. 1493.
The first Prayer Book, however, forbad the Elevation, which is here depicted.

Church practice, and therefore inserted the Epiklesis into the prayer *Quam oblationem*, while at the same time forbidding the Elevation. In the Eastern Liturgies, as well as in our own Scottish and American Liturgies, the Epiklesis comes *after* the so-called words of Institution; but, by inserting them before these words in the First Prayer Book, Cranmer attempted a reconciliation between the Eastern and Western ideas.

It is important to remember that neither theory of consecration is primitive. See pp. 184–94.

The Prayer of Consecration is followed by 'Wherefore, O Lorde and heavenly father, accordyng to the Instytucyon of thy derely beloved sonne', &c. (the *Unde et memores* of the Latin rites), continuing, 'And here wee offre and present unto thee (O Lorde) oure selfe, oure soules', &c. (our Prayer of Oblation). The Lord's Prayer comes next, and then 'Christ our Pascall lambe is offred up for us,' &c.: after which is inserted the Order of the Communion, from 'You that do truly' to the Words of Administration. The *Agnus Dei* (of course in English) is ordered to be sung during the Communion, and after it are twenty-two sentences from the New Testament, one of which is to be said or sung as a post-Communion. These are followed by our Prayer of Thanksgiving, and the Blessing.

Occasional Services

The Baptismal Services contain, besides the parts which we are familiar with, an Exorcism of the 'uncleane spirite', and a rubric for thrice dipping the child in the water (which is ordered to be changed once a month, and the new water blessed): but the pouring of water is allowed if the child be weak. After this, the sponsors are to take the child, and the minister to put on him his white vesture, commonly called the Chrisom, with the words 'Take this white vesture for a token of the innocencie', &c.; and the priest anoints the infant upon the head. The chrisom is to be brought back at the mother's churching.

The Catechism is printed under the head of Confirmation, and ends at the Lord's Prayer and the Desire. At Confirmation the Bishop not only lays his hand upon every child, but crosses each child on the forehead (this was revived in the Scottish rite during the 18th century). The Visitation of the Sick contains a prayer and psalm for Unction, 'if the sicke person desyre to be annoynted'; and the Communion of the Sick appoints that if on the day appointed 'there be a celebracion of the holy communion in the churche, then shall the priest reserve (at the open communion) so muche of the sacrament of the body and bloud, as shall serve'. For Burial, the Psalms are 116, 146, 139 (a better selection than those of 1662); and there is a beautiful commendation and a prayer for the departed person 'that his soule and all the soules of thy electe, departed out of this lyfe, may with us and we with them, fully receive thy promisses, and be made perfite altogether'. The prayer 'Almighty God, with whom do live' is differently worded; and then follow an Introit (Psalm 42), Collect ('O merciful God', rather more definitely worded), Epistle, and Gospel, for funeral Celebrations.

After Churching and the Commination, the First Prayer Book concludes with what is now our third preface, and 'Certayne Notes for the more playne explicacion and decent ministracion of thinges conteined in thys booke'. The first Note orders the surplice and allows the hood for Mattins, Evensong, Baptizing, and Burying (a rubric before the Holy Communion orders the

19. THE ALBE AND VESTMENT

Brass at Saffron Walden.

Over his apparelled amice and albe, the priest wears a 'vestment', i.e. a stole and fanon which are embroidered with the same pattern as the apparels, and a perfectly plain chasuble, large and bell-shaped and gathered into ample folds at the arms, so that it is very like the paenula on pp. 69 and 202.

albe, vestment or cope, and tunicle for that service). The second Note appoints the rochet, surplice, or albe, cope or vestment, and the pastoral staff for the Bishop—but not the mitre: Cranmer celebrated without his, at St. Paul's on July 21st, 1549. The third is—'As touching kneeling, crossing, holding up of handes, knocking upon the brest, and other gestures: they may be used or left as every man's devocion serveth without blame'. The fourth allows the singing of an anthem instead of the Litany on the Great Feasts; and the fifth gives the curate discretion to omit the Litany, *Gloria in Excelsis*, Creed, Homily, and Exhortation, 'if there bee a sermone, or for other greate cause'.

These Notes well illustrate that common sense which is characteristic of the First Prayer Book. It is indeed throughout an exemplar of what we proudly claim as one of the best elements in the English character: alike in ritual, that is, in the wording of the services, and in ceremonial, it endeavours to avoid the extremes of bigots and fanatics, seeking to establish what is true and right without regard to prejudices, reactions, and the cruel generalizations so characteristic of religious controversy. Catholic conservatism there is, but it is the conservatism which is not afraid of new ideas; Protestantism there is, but it is the Protestantism that will not throw away the gold with the dross; compromise there is, but it is the compromise which honestly accepts truth from both sides. It is positive, constructive, practical; and, though some of its provisions are no longer needed at the present time, every subsequent revision so far has restored something which the Second Book took away. In fact, as is stated in the very Act which substituted the Second Book for it, the First Prayer Book was 'a very godly order ... for common prayer and administration of the sacraments, ... agreeable to the word of God and the primitive Church'; but there had 'arisen in the use and exercise . . . . divers doubts for the fashion and manner of the ministration of the same, rather by curiosity of the minister, and mistakers, than of any other worthy cause'. The First Prayer Book was indeed too fair-minded for the violent and bitter spirit of the age.

Our Book of Common Prayer has been like a ship launched upon a troublous sea. The ship was shattered before the end of this reign, sunk in that of Mary, refitted when Elizabeth began to reign, wrecked in the storms of the 17th century, then careened and repaired: she was becalmed in the 18th, until the American Book was made; then, after steering a gusty course between the rocks of the Victorian era, the English Book has become, now in the 20th century, the oldest ship of a small fleet, tough and full of life in spite of her age, and sailing with a good wind, but needing again the shipwright's hand.

CHAPTER VII

THE SECOND PRAYER BOOK

THE First Prayer Book was too conservative for the foreign Reformers, some of whom had come to England—notably Bucer, of Strassburg, and Peter Martyr Vermigli, an Italian, who were installed at Cambridge and Oxford respectively as divinity professors—while others, including Calvin himself ('the Geneva Pope'), who was graciously pleased to say that the Book contained 'many tolerable absurdities', sent letters calling for more drastic changes. The criticisms of these and other of the more extreme men, such as Hooper, the Bishop of Gloucester, and Ridley—who had been given the See of London, of which Bonner was deprived by the Council of Regency—had great influence upon the singularly open mind of Cranmer. Almost from the moment the First Prayer Book was published, measures were being taken for superseding it by another book which should be more acceptable to the Continental Reformers and the small but determined body of extremists in England.

Meanwhile, the reign of Henry VIII (who always acted with the consent of Parliament) had been succeeded by a despotism of anarchy under the boy-king. Bonner and Gardiner were now in prison—they were to have their revenge in Mary's reign; all moderates and conservatives were removed from the Council, and the moderate bishops from their sees. The first Protector, Somerset, had endeavoured, with Cranmer and Latimer, to redeem the miseries of the poor, and he was a premature apostle of religious toleration; but even Somerset was a hearty robber, as the name of Somerset House may remind us. To build there a palace (which he did not live to enjoy) he destroyed three bishops' houses and one parish church, as if they had been so much slum property; and he pulled down the cloister of St. Paul's Cathedral and Clerkenwell Priory for further building materials. The story, however, that he had actually intended to build his palace on the site of Westminster Abbey, and was only held back by the offer of half the Abbey's estates, has never been substantiated. Somerset was sent to the Tower in the year of the First Prayer Book, to be beheaded two years afterwards. His successor, Northumberland, was a villain unmitigated. The misery of the poor increased, the character of

20. BISHOP HOOPER

the clergy did not improve: 'ass-heads' and 'lack-Latins' still abounded, as the immortal sermons of Latimer bear witness.

The destruction of the altars in London by Ridley was at least conscientious, though it was illegal, as well as barbarous and unreasonable (the Lutherans were sensible enough to spare the beautiful altar-pieces of Germany and Scandinavia, and their Protestantism did not suffer thereby); but the Council sent officials all over the country who looted for the sake of plunder—the organs were sold for the price of their pipes, even the melting of the bells was begun; the priceless church plate, which had been the treasure of the people for centuries, was seized, so that, a generation later, there were still some churches with nothing but a single chalice. The parish churches, as well as the benefit clubs and guilds, had belonged to the people; but now Commissioners were sent all over England to make inventories, 'forasmuch as the King's Majesty had need presently of a mass of money'; and before the end of poor little King Edward's reign there had been a clean sweep of all that was worth stealing: the churches, their chests, their treasuries had been ransacked. In some places the roofs and even the walls were suffered to decay.

21. A 'STABLE OF ASSES'
TOM TOWER, CHRIST CHURCH, OXFORD

In the Second Book of Homilies, issued in Queen Elizabeth's reign, nine years after King Edward's death, we read: 'It is a sin and shame to see so many churches so ruinous and so foully decayed, almost in every corner. . . . Suffer them not to be defiled with rain and weather, with dung of doves and owls, stares and choughs, and other filthiness, and as it is foul and lamentable to behold in many places of this country.' The hospitals and almshouses were destroyed; the universities only just escaped. 'To the Universities', says J. A. Froude, 'the Reformation brought with it desolation. .... They were called Stables of Asses. . . . The Government cancelled the exhibitions which had been granted for the support of poor scholars. They suppressed the Professorships and Lectureships. . . . College Libraries were plundered and burnt. The Divinity Schools at Oxford were planted with cabbages, and the laundresses dried clothes in the School of Arts.' It was not the Dissolution of the Monasteries under Henry that helped to make pauperism out of the break-up of the Feudal system, but the Disendowment of the Parishes under his son. The bulk of the money went to enrich the gang of ruffians who tyrannized over England: the thirty 'King Edward VI Schools' really owe nothing to him or his government, as Gairdner has shown. The old parish community was destroyed; 'an atmosphere of meanness and squalor', wrote Dr. Jessopp at the close of the Victorian era, still pervades 'the shrivelled assemblies' of the 17th and 18th centuries; though now, in the 20th, both Parish Councils and Parochial Church Councils have been established by Act of Parliament in England.

Thus, side by side with the influence of the genuine reformers, and of the extremists, and of the foreigners—some of whom, including Bucer, the most prominent critic, could not speak a word of the language in which the Prayer Book was written— was the brigandage of men like Northumberland, who had no zeal for Protestantism—indeed, Northumberland professed himself a Papist on the scaffold. The Edwardian robbers were not genuine reformers, but they effectively helped to destroy the old manner of worship which had gone on under the First Prayer Book by their looting of the ornaments. They began the work of destruction; still more was done in the next century by the Puritans. The actual buildings, however, did not suffer much till the 19th century.

THE SECOND BOOK

In 1552 Parliament passed the Act above mentioned, which stated that the First Prayer Book was agreeable to the Word of God, but that doubts had arisen (through curiosity rather than any worthy cause), and it would therefore be explained and made perfect. Thus, in 1532, the Second Prayer Book appeared, but without any sanction from the Convocations.

There were many changes. Besides adding the now obsolete Prayers in time of Dearth, War, and Famine, and introducing the Decalogue into the Communion Service, it also added the penitential introduction to Mattins and Evensong, which services in the First Book had begun with the Lord's Prayer. Ruskin had some justification when, in his *Letters to the Clergy*, he complained of people having to pray in the morning that the rest of their lives should be pure and holy, when they knew that a few hours later they would be required to say that there was no health in them. This remained the order for every day in the year; and it was only the 'Dearly beloved brethren' that the Shortened Services Act of 1872 allowed to be dropped on week-days. The American Prayer Book gives a wide liberty to omit on normal occasions this penitential Introduction, and, like the Scottish Book, relaxes considerably the obligation to read the Decalogue. The other revisions have moved in the same direction.

Exorcism was rightly omitted from the Baptismal Service; the rites for anointing the sick, and for taking the Sacrament to them from the open Communion, were with less reason omitted from the Visitation; and the provision of a special Celebration was omitted from the Burial Service, while the prayers for the departed were made vaguer. The 'Black

22. THE VESTMENT FORBIDDEN, 1532-3
An effigy in Wells Cathedral

A 13th-century bishop wearing vestments and a plain round cap. The vestment or chasuble must have looked much like a full surplice when it was white; it was evidently of thin material, as is that on p. 61, which is two centuries later. This historical garment, originally called *phelonion* or *paenula*, hardly changed for over a thousand years—from before the 5th century (see the figure on p. 202) to the 15th. It is mentioned as an overcoat (*phailonen*) in 2 Tim. 4: 13, and was originally circular in shape. Although covered by the Ornaments Rubric from the reign of Elizabeth onwards, it was never used again after 1559 for the Prayer-Book service till the 19th century.

Rubric' (see p. 117) was pasted into the book at the last moment.

More noticeable were the changes in matters of ceremonial. Morning and Evening Prayer were to be 'in such place . . . as the people may best hear'—that is, in any part of the church that the fancy of the minister might suggest. The anointing, the chrisom-vesture, and the triple repetition of the immersion were removed from the Baptismal Service, and the rubric as to the bread and wine and water from the Communion. Two ceremonies of late origin—the delivery of the chalice to the priest and of his pastoral staff to the bishop—were omitted from the Ordinal. But the outward character of the services, in the churches which the Commissioners were fleecing, was most affected by the disappearance of the former rubrics and notes ordering the old vestments, and by a new rubric stating that neither albe, vestment, nor cope should be worn, but that the bishop should wear a rochet and the priest a surplice only— the innocuous hood and scarf thus sharing the fate of the other garments.

The Liturgy. The Second Model

The most important changes of 1552 were those in the Service of Holy Communion. In this, the Second Model, as we will call it, Archbishop Cranmer set forth his matured conclusions. It is a mistake to think that in this and in other things the First Book was beyond improvement; but many consider that the changes were too drastic, especially the alleged removal of the Epiklesis, which we have already mentioned on p. 58. The addition of the Decalogue had probably more justification then than now, when there is a general preference for the Summary of the Law, as it is given in the Scottish and American Liturgies. The American, however, combines much of the Second Model with the First.

Proud as we are of the First Model, there is no less cause for pride in the Second, when we remember that its purpose is to provide a liturgy that is Apostolic rather than Patristic. The omission of the Introits, the *Benedictus*, and the *Agnus* is an advantage in which the First Model in its present use now shares (for they are no longer anywhere compulsory). It was a good change; and even those who like to use these forms in the place of anthems or hymns, as is generally allowed to be legitimate, would not desire to have them all made compulsory again.

23. BISHOP LATIMER

In the Second Model the Eucharistic Prayer (the Canon) is divided into five parts, the Church Militant Prayer being separated from *Lift up your hearts* by the Exhortations, &c., and the *Sanctus* separated from the Prayer of Consecration by the Prayer of Access, while the Lord's Prayer comes after the Communion, and another part is placed in the Prayer of Oblation. This has been much criticized by those who are strongly influenced by Medieval precedent; but as a matter of fact there is precedent in the Gallican rites; and it may fairly be said that the division of a long prayer into shorter forms makes the whole much easier to follow, and therefore that it is easier for the people to pray, which is after all the chief consideration in a service. It may also be argued that the use of one long prayer was always a liturgical mistake, and that it is better liturgical art to have a looser texture (to borrow an analogy from painting), and that the whole 'shape' and significance of the service is thereby improved.

There is a real danger in attaching too much importance to Patristic or Medieval forms. The Latin canon especially had been too long, and unbroken—for it was not relieved by responses and choruses as the Eastern Liturgies are. It is in itself a rather unskilful piece of patchwork; and, though it is much older than the Medieval ideas it was supposed to represent, and is indeed an interesting witness against those exaggerations, in its comparative sobriety and moderation, it could never be properly followed by the people—indeed it can seldom have been really understood by the priest himself, and the meaning of some parts is still obscure. Cumbrous and long-drawn, it is only made possible by being rapidly and inaudibly muttered; and when the service is sung to a modern 'mass', the music overlaps and obscures it.

To those who are used to other forms, the ending of the Eucharistic Prayer may seem abrupt. But Cranmer may have been influenced by the Liturgy of St. Chrysostom; for in that also the words over the bread and over the cup are each immediately followed by 'Amen', though the long prayer does go on. There is impressiveness and force in this sudden transition into the silence; and those churches which observe a complete break for some moments at this point bear unconscious witness to the value of the liturgical device. And surely it was the inspiration of a great liturgical artist to move the *Gloria in excelsis* from its awkward place at the beginning of the service, and to make it the splendid dramatic climax that it is in the Second Model, and indeed in all subsequent revisions throughout the Anglican Church.

'What Cranmer did', says Professor Burkitt, 'and what is still done in the English Church, is to interlace the consecration and oblation of the Sacrament with the communion of clergy and people. In all other Liturgies they are separate.' This is a change of the greatest value. Cranmer was 'a sound Latin liturgist, and had also studied the Greek rite; he did not go in the direction of Geneva, but in that of St. Augustine'. 'The sacrifice in the Eucharist was to be retained, not done away with, as contemporary Protestants demanded, but it was to be the sacrifice of Christians offering themselves.' This is the reason for the interlacing. The Prayer of Oblation comes after the Communion: the sacrifice is that of those already united in the communion and fellowship of the Body of Christ.

There is yet one more important reason why scholars like Dr. J. W. Hunkin call it 'the best service for the Holy Communion in the whole of Christendom': it is 'the form most patient of interpretation in the light of modern study and research'. The documents that have been discovered in recent years about the Early Church and the great progress in New Testament criticism have in many ways strengthened the case for the Second Model. Briefly it may be said that, while the First Model is valuable because it is more in accord with the early liturgical forms that begin to appear about the time of St. Athanasius (see p. 198), the Second Model is nearer to the practice and belief of the Apostolic age. It is after all of the first importance that we should have a form that can be reconciled with what St. Paul intended and what can be gathered from the Evangelists. To find fault with the Prayer of Consecration because it does not follow the First Model is beside the point; for Cranmer's whole idea was to provide a different form which should be more in accord with the New Testament.

Many have discussed the Prayer of Consecration without observing that from beginning to end it is just one complete sentence, of which the predicate is 'Grant that we receiving these thy creatures . . . may be partakers of'. It is itself an Epiklesis; but the Epiklesis has been made personal, as it

24. THE LAST DAYS OF CRANMER

From Foxe's *Book of Martyrs.*

Dr. Cole is disputing with him from a pulpit. A friar and a graduate are pulling him from a platform. The two figures on the left are priests in gown, tippet, and cap. Cranmer is not dressed as a bishop. He let his beard grow after the death of Henry VIII.

was in the Early Church (see pp. 184, 194, 200). This is not the Medieval doctrine; but it is what St. Paul teaches when he says, 'The cup of blessing which we bless, is it not a participation in the blood of Christ? The bread which we break, is it not a participation in the body of Christ?' And it very carefully avoids going further than St. Paul.

The End of the Reign

In May, 1552, the Privy Council had published Forty-two Articles which endeavoured to enforce some of the doctrines of the Continental Reformers upon the English Church. Article 42 condemned those 'who endeavour at this time to restore the dangerous opinion that all men, be they never so ungodly, shall at length be saved'. As in the case of the Second Prayer Book, the English Church was not invited to sanction these Articles; but the Council had the effrontery to state on the title-page that they had been agreed upon by the bishops in Convocation. By November 1st the Second Prayer Book was ready for use; and it remained in force for eight months—till the end of the reign.

The looting went on, as the Second Prayer Book ran through its brief career. Early in 1553, a new commission was issued, directing the seizure of all remaining valuables from the churches: the plate was sent to the Tower of London, and melted down, 'forasmuch as the King's Majesty' was still in that mysterious need 'of a mass of money'. Poor little King! On July 6th he was dead; and England showed her opinion of the deeds that had been done in his name, by welcoming with enthusiasm Queen Mary to his throne. Poor Mary, poor England! The chief actors of the former reign pass away to prison or exile, or to the bitter vengeance of the faggot and the axe.

SUMMARY OF EVENTS

1549. MARCH. **The First English Prayer Book.**
   SEPTEMBER. Deprivation of Bonner, Bishop of London, followed later by that of other bishops.
   OCTOBER. Fall of the Protector Somerset. Northumberland rules the Council of Regency.
1549–52. Bucer, Peter Martyr, Calvin, and others put forward objections to the First Prayer Book.

1550. *The First English Ordinal.*

Destruction of altars by Bishop Ridley in London.

1552. Various 'Commissions for Church Goods'.

APRIL. The Second Act of Uniformity sanctions the new Prayer Book.

MAY. The Forty-two Articles.

NOVEMBER 1ST. **The Second English Prayer Book** first used.

1553. JANUARY. Last Edwardian Commission for Church goods.

JULY 6TH. Death of King Edward VI. Accession of Queen Mary. Execution of the Protector Northumberland (who now declares himself a Papist after all).

1554. Reconciliation of England to the Papacy.

1555–8. The Marian Persecutions. Martyrdom of Cranmer, Latimer, Ridley, Hooper, and about 300 others.

1558. Accession of Queen Elizabeth.

CHAPTER VIII

THE ELIZABETHAN PRAYER BOOK

MERCIFULLY we can pass over the horrors of the Marian persecutions, whose only effect was to stiffen the broad back of England against the Pope, and profoundly to deepen our national Protestantism. We are concerned here only with the history of a single book, and we therefore turn at once to the Third Act of Uniformity, in the year after Elizabeth's accession.

The Latin services had of course been used in Mary's reign. She had restored the Sarum rites: the Roman ritual was not introduced among the English Papists till early in the 17th century. On November 17th, 1558, Elizabeth came to the throne; and measures were at once taken for the restoration

25. QUEEN ELIZABETH
From the painting by Zucchero in the National Portrait Gallery.

of the Prayer Book. Queen Elizabeth, who sided with the small but sensible moderate party, was determined that the Second Book should be relieved of its more extreme features. In April, 1559, the Elizabethan Act of Uniformity was passed, nine bishops voting against it : the *Third Prayer Book*, thus introduced, met with little opposition, and led to the deprivation of only about 200 of the Marian clergy. Convocation had not been consulted. The consent of the Church can thus only be claimed by virtue of its subsequent acquiescence; but from this time the history of the Prayer Book as a national institution may fairly be said to begin.

In thus restoring the Second Book and what we have called the Second Model for the Liturgy, certain few but important alterations were secured, which made the Elizabethan Prayer Book very different in effect. The chief changes in the Third Prayer Book were as follows:

PRINCIPAL CHANGES IN THE ELIZABETHAN PRAYER BOOK

Morning and Evening Prayer were to be 'in the accustomed place', i.e. in the choir, instead of 'in such place . . . as the people may best hear'. The next rubric of the Second Book, forbidding all vestments but the rochet and surplice, was superseded by the Ornaments Rubric, which brought back at one stroke the externals of public worship to the condition under the First Book (p. 61), ordering the minister to 'use such ornaments in the church as were in use by authority of parliament in the second year of the reign of king Edward the VI'.

In the Communion, the old words of administration, 'The Body of our Lord', &c., were restored: but the sentence of the Second Book, 'Take and eat this', &c., was left in as well, and thus the form became too long. The Black Rubric was removed. The Prayer for the Queen and the Prayer for Clergy and People were added, but they were printed at the end of the Litany: the mistake of printing the 'State Prayers' (with that for the Royal Family, added in 1604) as if they were obliged to be used, apparently, twice a day was not made till 1662 (p. 115). The few other changes were of little importance: but it is a credit to Elizabethan statesmanship that, when the embers of Smithfield were hardly cooled, the petition to be delivered 'from the tyranny of the bishop of Rome, and all his detestable enormities' was removed from the Litany.

In 1560 a Latin Version of the Prayer Book was published, and in the same year was issued the first of those Additional Services by which our worship has been enriched from time to time in succeeding ages. These have been mentioned on p. 41, but constant misapprehensions make it worth repeating that neither the Prayer Book itself nor the Act of Uniformity enforcing it prevent the use of duly authorized additional services.

26. ALTAR OF THE BLESSED VIRGIN IN KING HENRY THE SEVENTH'S CHAPEL, WESTMINSTER ABBEY

Under which Edward VI was buried. It was set up by Henry VIII, and was destroyed by the Puritans in 1643. The two pilasters which are seen supporting the ends of the altar were afterwards found, and are now restored to the present altar.

In 1561 a Commission was appointed to revise the Kalendar, and the names of the black-letter saints, much as we now have them, were added. In 1562 the Forty-two Articles were reduced to Thirty-nine;

and Article 42, which had asserted the existence of Hell in terms very moderate for the times, disappeared for ever.

In the same year the Pope forbade his adherents to attend the English services, and in 1570 he launched his Bull of Excommunication, *Regnans in excelsis*, against Queen Elizabeth, and thus finally separated them from the English Church.

In 1571 the Second Book of Homilies was issued. In 1594 Richard Hooker issued the first books of his *Ecclesiastical Polity*, a classic 'never surpassed', as Saintsbury says, 'and hardly ever equalled', wherein he set out the magnificent ideal of a Church broad enough and tolerant enough to win the adherence of all good Englishmen. His tolerance however was before its time. Perhaps we are approaching it to-day.

PURITAN OPPOSITION

Meanwhile the Puritans struggled to have the Prayer Book altered, and many evaded its use. The return of the Marian exiles increased their power; and efforts were made, in Convocation and in Parliament, to abolish those beautiful and helpful ceremonies which stirred some men to a strangeness of opposition in this era of religious reaction. The sign of the cross in Baptism, kneeling at communion, the wedding-ring, every sort of vestment, including the black gown and college cap as well as the cope and surplice, were bitterly attacked. In 1562 a proposal in the lower house of Convocation to abolish these things, and also (incredible as it may seem to modern descendants of the Puritans) the organ, was only lost by one vote; and this was in spite of the known determination of the Queen, whose decisive action indeed alone prevented the House of Commons from perpetrating that wholesale vandalism.

We cannot understand the subsequent history of the Prayer Book unless we realize the strength of this feeling which fastened upon middle-class England. There was a good side to it. The Puritans (like St. Bernard) felt that the vision of God was obscured by decorative display. It is true also that excess of ornament is a real danger, and that beauty itself is lost when the need of simplicity and sincerity are forgotten. But there was also the insanity of a wild reaction, a kind of Romanism turned inside out. Because the Roman Catholic Church (in common with the whole of Christendom up to the 16th century) acted on the obvious truth that beauty is a good thing, the growing Puritan party paid Rome the compliment of embracing ugliness for her sake.

Many also in their theology, both Conformists and Nonconformists, embraced the dark side of medieval teaching, which had been evolved from the worst part of St. Augustine's thought, and they developed it under the guise of Calvinism into a system which was an insult not only to the beauty but also to the goodness of Almighty God. They taught that God had predestinated the vast majority of mankind to the torture of never ending fire (how merciful the fires of Smithfield in comparison!), not for any fault of their own—for, said the Lambeth Articles of 1595, 'God from eternity hath predestined some unto life and reprobated others unto death', and 'It is not placed within the will or power of every man to be saved'.

To-day, Churchmen and Nonconformists alike repudiate this most terrible of human errors. At the very height of the Puritan reaction there were men like Milton who were not Calvinists— Milton was indeed an Arian, and not therefore orthodox from either point of view. But, none the less, Calvinism was the creed that was set up against the teaching of the Church; Calvinism was the creed of the Puritan party, though indeed men like Richard Baxter held it in a modified form; and it was the power of Calvinism that was to bring King Charles I and Archbishop Laud to the block. Yet with Calvinism there were identified many great and noble qualities, and the struggle of

Puritanism against royal absolutism was a real struggle for human freedom.

We must imagine ourselves therefore on the eve of the 17th century. Puritanism has been growing throughout Elizabeth's reign. The greatest men—Shakespeare, for instance—stood contemptuously aside from the 'precisians', and the great Elizabethan era went its own way, worshipped its Queen, and admired its Prayer Book. But the middle class, brought up on Foxe's *Book of Martyrs* and the Geneva Bible (p. 90), was largely Puritan; many of the bishops withstood the Queen in the interests of Puritanism as much as they dared; they had long since pulled down the altars. Its power was still to increase, and it was absorbing much that was strongest and best in England. Already some used the Prayer Book in a mutilated form: it was, said the anonymous *First Admonition to Parliament*, which was attributed to the greatest of the Elizabethan Puritans, Thomas Cartwright, 'an unperfect book, culled and picked out of that Popish dunghill, the Portuise [breviary] and Massbook, full of all abominations'. No one carried out in full the ceremonial directions of the English Church; and because the Ornaments Rubric was ignored, an attempt has been made in 1566 by the issue of the 'Advertisements' to secure at least

M. THO: CARTWRIGHT

27. From a contemporary print.

the minimum of conformity—the surplice, hood, and cope, with the frontal and fair linen for the holy Table.

At the present day the Anglican Church is the great standing witness to the world against the notion we have described—

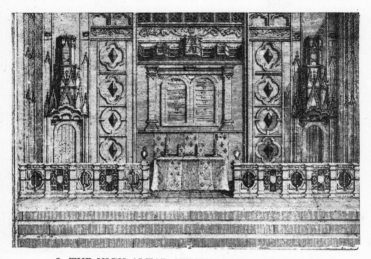

28. THE HIGH ALTAR, WINCHESTER CATHEDRAL
In the 17th century.
The altar has a frontal and dorsal with orphreys embroidered with fleurs-de-lis; on it are the Gospeller's and Epistoler's Books, and two candles.

that beauty is a monopoly of the Churches in communion with Rome, or Constantinople. It is no longer a party matter to promote beauty in worship through the order and ornaments of the Prayer Book.

But in the 16th and 17th centuries all this was not possible. The most the Church could do was to fight hard for the very idea of liturgical worship, and for a few things that preserved the principle of ceremonial, modest as they were—such as the surplice, the cope in great churches, the organ, the vested altar, the cross in baptism, kneeling for communion, and the wedding-ring.

They misjudge the Church of England who blame her because sometimes her worship has lacked order and beauty, while in some places, by a not unnatural reaction, unlawful eccentricities have arisen. If she had not taken in nearly all her sail once, she would not have come through the storms at all. She had to let secondary things go, in order that she might preserve the essentials of that holy spirit of prayer which is the heritage of historic Christianity; and her patient spirit of tolerance is amply vindicated to-day.

SUMMARY OF EVENTS

1558. NOVEMBER. Accession of Elizabeth.

1559. APRIL. **Third Prayer Book** and Third Act of Uniformity.

1560. First of many Additional Services issued.

1561. The Kalendar revised.

Day's 'Partial Psalter', the *Old Version* (Sternhold and Hopkins), with some additional hymns, and the Queen's interim licence for private use.

1562. The Thirty-nine Articles. (Hell is removed, and some other things, from the original Forty-two.)

The Pope withdraws his adherents from the Church services, and thus begins the schism between England and Rome.

Day's 'Complete Psalter', the *Old Version* as above, in almost its final form, with the Queen's seven years' licence for private use.

1566. The Advertisements enforce a minimum of ceremonial.

The *Old Version*, as above, printed by Day with the Queen's licence, and 'allowed to be sung of the people, in Churches, before and after Morning and Evening prayer: as also before and after the Sermon, and moreover in private houses'.

1571. Second Book of Homilies.

1603. MARCH. Accession of James I.

CHAPTER IX

THE HAMPTON COURT CONFERENCE AND THE FOURTH PRAYER BOOK

A SUBJECT has many sides, and while we blame a party for its action on one side we may have to praise it for the good it wrought upon another. No praise can be too high for the Puritans in their zeal for the Bible as they understood it. Indeed the English Bible was and is the common ground of Anglicans and Nonconformists, the chief glory of the English Reformation. 'For my part,' Gladstone once wrote, 'without going farther, I see in the free use of Scripture by the Christian people at large, not for controversy, nor for dogmatic accuracy, nor for the satisfaction of the understanding, but for its milk and meat, the food of the spirit—one undeniable object and fruit of the English Reformation.'

Unfortunately we may not linger here for long in the consideration of this great subject, since we are only concerned in this history with the Bible as the rock from which the Prayer Book was hewn and upon which it stands. For the wider aspect of the matter let us be content with another extract—this time from a great German historian. Dr. Döllinger says: 'I believe we may credit one great superiority in England over other countries to the circumstance that there the Holy Scripture is found in every house, as is the case nowhere else in the world. It is, so to speak, the good genius of the place, the protecting spirit of the domestic hearth and family.'

So it is that when as historians we look back upon the past, we see good in both sides of the old controversies. It was the good indeed that made each party live; for no party lives except for the good in it, and the evil is but lumber that it carries.

Those who come after—some time after—are able to separate the good from the evil, and to possess all that is worthy, not from one side only, but from both. Thus the world does slowly grow in wisdom, learning to eschew what is evil and to hold fast what is good. We in this little history may well condemn the evil done by a small gang of robbers in the reign of Edward VI, the narrowness of Puritanism, the arrogance and bitterness of both sides; but Puritanism destroyed for us ancient and deep-rooted evils, and helped us to win that freedom to-day which is the main hope of Christendom—the freedom to go back behind the traditions of men to the plain words and pure example of our Lord Jesus Christ.

THE HAMPTON COURT CONFERENCE

When James I came to the throne, the Puritans drew up a 'Millenary Petition' for reform; and as a result the Hampton Court Conference (1604) was held by the King, who loved disputations above all things. The familiar petty objections were raised to the cross in Baptism, to the square cap, and the surplice ('a kind of garment', said they, 'which the priests of Isis used to wear'); the wedding-ring, the word 'priest', bowing at the name of Jesus; the Puritans also disliked the Thirty-nine Articles as not sanctioning Calvinism and Hell; they desired that Baptism should never be ministered by women, that Confirmation should be taken away, and also the Churching of Women, that 'examination' should go before Communion, that 'the longsomeness of service' should be 'abridged' and 'Church songs and music moderated', that the Lord's Day should not be 'profaned' (by the playing of games), that a uniformity of doctrine should be prescribed, and a few other things. Some of these requests (especially that for uniformity) were very bad indeed, and few would be defended to-day: even that against 'longsomeness', we fear, was only to gain more room for sermons and extempore prayers that were more longsome still.

King James, who so loved an argument, enjoyed the Hampton Court Conference very much. He wrote afterwards that he had peppered the Puritans—in his own inimitable words: 'We

have kept such a revell with the Puritans here this two days, as was never heard the like: quhaire I have peppered thaime as soundlie as yee have done the Papists thaire. . . . They fled me so from argument to argument, without ever answering me directly, *ut est eorum moris*, as I was forced at last to say unto thaime; that if any of thaime had been in a college disputing with their scholars, if any of thair disciples had answered them in that sort, they would have fetched him up in a place of a reply; and so should the rod have plyed upon the poor boyes buttocks.'

29. KING JAMES I
From a painting by Paul van Somer in the National Portrait Gallery.

Poor disputants! we can see James smiling and stammering his triumph at their courtly retreat. That retreat was not to be for long.

THE FOURTH PRAYER BOOK

In February, 1604, less than a month after the Hampton Court Conference, the Fourth or Jacobean Prayer Book was issued. It did not contain very important alterations, and did little to satisfy the Puritans; but, unlike its two immediate predecessors, it had the direct sanction of Convocation, which in the new Canons of 1604 ordered it to be used.

Vera Effigies Reverendi in Cristo Patris Dni. IOH: OVERALL. Episcopi Norwicensis.

I.V. Hollar fec
[illegible]

30. DR. OVERALL

One of the revisers of 1604, and of the translators of the Bible in 1607–11. He was afterwards Bishop of Norwich.

The most important addition was the fifth part of the Catechism, that ample concluding section which so admirably defines the Sacraments; this is supposed to have been written by Dr. Overall. The Prayer for the Royal Family—which has been felt since by some to increase the longsomeness of Divine Service—was added, though only at the end of the Litany; and the Thanksgivings for Rain, Fair Weather, Plenty, Peace, Deliverance from the Plague, were also put in. On the other hand, to please the Puritans who disapproved of the possibility of feminine ministrations, Private Baptism was restricted to a 'lawful Minister' (a term which, strictly understood, does not exclude lay Baptism in case of necessity); the explanatory sub-title to Confirmation, 'Or laying on of hands', &c., was added; and similarly to the title 'The Absolution' were joined the words 'or Remission of sins'. The Puritans had demanded the abolition of all Lessons from the Apocrypha (some of which are of extreme value and beauty); and as a concession, the quaint history of Bel and the Dragon, and the much-loved romance of Tobit were given up.

In the same year the Canons of 1604, which had been drawn up by Convocation in 1603, received the sanction of the Crown. These Canons pronounced excommunication upon those, whether Puritans or Romanists, who 'impugned' the Prayer Book or refused to use it, and they asserted the historical claim of the English Church to be a part of the Church Catholic. They affected our ritual by enforcing once again the Bidding Prayer before Sermons, and our ceremonial by ordering the reverence at the name of Jesus, and certain minimum requirements of the Ornaments Rubric—the altar frontal and fair linen, the cope, surplice, hood, tippet (i.e. scarf), and the square cap with cassock and gown, and tippet or hood, out of doors.

CHAPTER X

THE AUTHORIZED VERSION OF THE BIBLE

AT the Hampton Court Conference, the learned leader of the Puritan party, Dr. Reynolds, proposed a revision of the Bible. In doing so, he aimed at Puritanism—unconsciously, no doubt—the greatest blow it could possibly receive; for the very source and soil of it was the Geneva Bible of 1560 (known now to collectors as the Breeches Bible because of its translation of Gen. 3: 7, 'The eyes of them bothe were opened, and they sewed figge-tree leaves together, and made themselves breeches'), which—printed in modern type instead of black letter—was the popular version of the English people; and, being full of Calvinistic notes, and bound up with a Calvinistic Catechism, spread everywhere the tenets of the Genevan teacher. This fact could not have occurred to the Anglicans present, for the proposal to prepare a new version was ill received.

One man, however, took up the idea with enthusiasm, and this was the King himself, to whom the first credit of our English Bible is due. Was it that he alone had the shrewdness to see that the impracticable Bishops' Bible of 1568 could never supplant the Geneva Bible, and that Puritanism would continue to spread unless an impartial version of the Scriptures was produced? It may well have been so; for we have James's own words as to his hatred of the Geneva Bible, with its 'notes very partial, untrue, seditious, and savouring too much of dangerous and traitorous conceits'. His scholar's instinct was aroused as well; 'for he could never yet see a Bible well translated in English, but the worst of all his Majesty thought the Geneva to be'.

After the Conference was over, King James drew up a list

of fifty-four divines. It is to be remarked that none of them were bishops at the time, though some were made bishops afterwards: the Authorized Version, in fact, owes its excellence to the common sense of the King in choosing his men for their learning and capacity, and not for their official position. This may seem a very obvious piece of wisdom: but it is to be noted that it has been forgotten by the English authorities in the hitherto unsuccessful 20th-century attempts at Prayer Book revision. King James's fifty-four divines were afterwards reduced to the 'prodigiously learned and earnest persons, forty-seven in number', who, Carlyle says, gave us our version of that Book of Books, 'which possesses this property, inclusive of all, add we, That it is written under the eye of the Eternal; that it is of a sincerity like very Death, the truest utterance that ever came by alphabetic letters from the Soul of Man'.

The English Bible like the English Prayer Book had had its baptism of blood. Men like Tyndale had been martyred for translating, printing, or circulating it; and now, when the generation that had wept over Tyndale and Cranmer was gone, Englishmen, who should have been united in a common cause, were heading for civil war. Yet it was in this age of strife that the uniting spirit of the Bible for a while prevailed. Puritans and High Churchmen had the Scriptures in common, and did alike fervently believe in them: outside the rooms in Oxford, Cambridge, and Westminster, where the forty-seven divines met, religious folk were maligning each other in brilliant, bitter, and abusive pamphlets; but within those learned conferences all hostilities were silenced, all differences ignored: men like Overall and the saintly Andrewes, on the one side, joined with Reynolds and Abbott on the other; and the forty-seven worked in such singular harmony that it is impossible to distinguish between the three companies which assembled in three different places: the Authorized Version of the Bible reads like the work of one great man.

The style varies indeed with the theme—the artless early histories, and the later, or Job and Ecclesiastes, with their sublimities of poetry, or the concise Wisdom Books of the canonical Scriptures and the Apocrypha, the calls and aspirations of Isaiah, the tears of Jeremiah, the visions of Ezekiel, the preaching of the Minor Prophets, the narrative simplicity of the Gospels and Acts, or those 'blazing passages in the Epistles, and the hues of sunset and eclipse that colour the Book of Revelation'. Yet through it all runs the constant music of what has been called the biblical cadence. The divines—who might have wrought a literary gem for the bookshelves of the learned, after the manner of the age that produced Donne and Milton, Burton and Sir Thomas Browne—

31. LANCELOT ANDREWES
One of the translators of the Bible. He was afterwards Bishop of Winchester.

threw aside the pedantries and preciosities which were in fashion, and sat humbly at the feet of those predecessors who in peril of death had hewn out the words of life with such strength of simplicity; and they produced a book which has been at once the comfort of the peasant and the model and inspiration of the hero, che poet, and the sage.

They were fine scholars. Scholars are not uncommon, and that was a very learned age. But it was also a great age of English literature: Shakespeare was just turned forty when King James appointed the Divines (it was the year of *Othello*, and two years after *Hamlet*); the second edition of Bacon's *Essays* was published a few months after those Divines had finished their work, and Milton was then in the fourth year of his precocious child-hood. Now scholars are not generally masters of prose, and the combination of the critical and the constructive gifts—of science and art—is rare to-day, when learned translations and exact commentaries are common enough, but the majority of ancient

32. DARTMOUTH PARISH CHURCH

Showing the magnificent pre-Reformation rood-screen and pulpit, with the rood restored.

books have still not been turned into English classics, and theology is seldom literature. The English Bible is an exception. We do not think of it as a translation at all: we think of it as the greatest of English classics, which, among other things, it is.

King James's forty-seven divines, appointed in 1604, got to work in 1607, and produced the Authorized Version of the Bible in 1611. When we consider their work and the earlier masterly exemplars whom they followed, Wyclif, Tyndale,

Coverdale, and the rest—when we contemplate the earnest courage, the humble faith, the perseverance of these men, and the undying majesty of their common offspring, we can only say that, if there is such a thing as the inspiration of the Bible, there has also been such a thing as an inspiration of those who translated it.

And what is true of the English Bible is true also of the English Prayer Book. Scholars who won the consecration of martyrdom gave to it a like power of inspired translation, and endowed it with the magic of their prose. Thus it is that the one book worthy to be set side by side with the English Bible is that Book of Common Prayer, which has won a place in the heart of the English-speaking nations second only to the Bible, and which day by day issues it forth in psalter and lectionary to the people.

ENGLISH VERSIONS OF THE BIBLE

7th to 14th centuries.

The Pioneers: Parts translated by Cædmon, Bede, Ælfric, and others (in Anglo-Saxon), Shoreham, Rolle, and others.

c. 1385.

Wyclif. Manuscript copies in Middle English, translated from the Latin. See p. 32.

(1476. Caxton introduces printing into England.)

1525.

Tyndale. New Testament, translated from the Greek. Also Pentateuch and Jonah, translated from the Hebrew.

1535.

Coverdale. The first complete printed Bible in English. Translated from the Latin and German, but based upon Tyndale.

1537.

Matthew's Bible. 'Matthew' is a pseudonym, and perhaps stands for Tyndale.

1539.

The Great Bible. (See p. 33.) By Coverdale, based on 'Matthew'. The 2nd edition (1540) and the five subsequent editions (1540–1) have a preface by Cranmer. The Prayer Book Psalter is from this Version.

1539.

Taverner's Bible. Little circulation or influence. A revision of 'Matthew'.

1560.

The Geneva Bible. The popular household Bible for a century, i.e. for long after the A.V. of 1611, because a handy volume, in roman type, and divided into verses. Made by the Protestant exiles in Geneva, and thus Calvinistic (p. 90), but scholarly, and of great influence on the A.V.

1568.

The Bishops' Bible. A revision of the Great Bible by Archbishop Parker and other bishops. A cumbersome book and no rival to the Genevan Bible, but the basis of the A.V.

1609.

The Douai Bible. The Roman Catholic Version. The New Testament was published at Rheims in 1582, the Old Testament at Douai in 1609. Closely follows the Latin.

1611.

The Authorized Version. Based on all previous translations, done by six committees, an Old Testament and a New Testament committee at Westminster, Oxford, and Cambridge.

1881–5.

The Revised Version. Done by a joint committee of Churchmen and Nonconformists. Not content with the corrections required by modern scholarship, the committee hampered itself with bad rules and produced a version inferior to the A.V., though valuable for reference and study.

CHAPTER XI
THE PURITANS IN POWER

THIS chapter must be short and gloomy. In 1637 a Scottish Prayer Book, with some improvements and a few concessions to Puritan feeling, was printed at Edinburgh. Its most distinctive features were due to the Scottish bishops, Maxwell of Ross and Wedderburn of Dunblane. Charles I favoured and influenced it. Archbishop Laud, who was always too high-handed, had wished to introduce the English Book into Scotland, and the Puritans succeeded in damaging the Scottish Book by coupling Laud's name with it also. This Scottish Book had afterwards considerable effect upon the last revision of the English in 1662, and was destined to give us the present Scottish Liturgy and the Liturgy of the American Church. But its tactless and arbitrary introduction in St. Giles, Edinburgh, in 1637 was made the occasion of a riot, when Jenny Geddes and other women threw their cutty-stools at the surpliced clergy, and the Bishop of Edinburgh barely escaped with his life. Not a minister in all Scotland dared use the book; and the overthrow of episcopacy followed soon after.

In 1640 a new code of Canons was issued by Laud, and sanctioned by King Charles, one of which enjoined bowing to the altar on entering and leaving the church; but in the same year the Long Parliament met, and condemned the Canons—among other things. In 1645 Laud was brought to the block to be followed four years later by his royal master. On the day of Laud's arrest, March 1st, 1641, a committee was appointed which demanded the abolition of altars, candlesticks, pictures and images, vestments, and the Ornaments Rubric by which they 'are now commanded', and many Church ceremonies; but

H

the destruction went further, and the bare condition of our churches a century ago was far more due to the Puritan icono-clasts than to the Edwardian robbers. The organs were burnt,

33. PURITAN PRESSURE

'A Fugitive for fear of this present Parliament.'

This woodcut, from a Puritan publication, 1641, represents the Vicar of Christ Church, Newgate Street, Edward Finch, leaving his parish because of 'charges exhibited in Parliament' against him. The Long Parliament met on November 3, 1640, and lasted, with vicissitudes, till 1660. Finch wears a hood and surplice over his cassock; and, holding a Prayer Book (doubtless), walks away from his church door. On a smaller scale he is shown in a coach 'away for hamersmith'.

the stained glass was smashed, the churches used to stable horses.

We get some idea of what was done by the records of the egregious Will Dowsing, who was the agent of the Cromwellian government for smashing churches at 6s. 8d. each: he has left us the proud record of his doings in parish after parish, and even notes with disgust that at one place he got only 3s. 4d., because there were no more than 'ten superstitious pictures and a cross' to be destroyed. This was at Hardwick, near Cambridge, in 1643. At the neighbouring village of Toft he expected more than his accustomed fee for a 'purification' of the church rather heavier than usual, but was disappointed, and got 'only 6s. 8d.' for destroying 'twenty-seven superstitious pictures in the

The Souldiers in their passage to York turn unto reformers pull down Popish pictures, break down rayles, turn altars into Tables

34. PURITAN ICONOCLASM
From a contemporary print.
One soldier is removing a cross from above the altar, while others carry off a picture and hew down the communion rails.

windows, ten others in stone [the beautiful alabaster reredos, fragments of which are still preserved in the church], three others in stone, three inscriptions, *Pray for the souls*, divers *Orate pro animabuses* [*sic*] in the windows, and a bell *Ora pro anima Sancta Katharina*'. At Queens', Cambridge, he tells us, 'we beat down a 110 superstitious pictures, besides Chirubims'; at Peterhouse, 'we pulled down two mighty great Angells with wings, and diverse other Angells, and the four Evangelists, and Peter with his Keies over the Chapell Dore, and about 100 Chirubims'; and the unhappy college authorities had to pay him themselves for ruining their chapels. It was only by some unknown private intervention (was it Milton himself who interceded with Cromwell?) that 'the storied windows richly dight', of King's College Chapel were spared to be the wonder of succeeding ages; for it is on record that the Bursar of King's paid the extra heavy fee for their destruction. These things need emphasizing; for the bareness of so many churches a century ago is commonly supposed to have been due to the English Church. It was due to her enemies; and was caused, not by the Prayer-Book system, but by the destruction of that system.

England lay under a military dictatorship which denied it the opportunity of telling its mind by a parliamentary election. Cromwell's followers are often praised as the pioneers of freedom: it is more exact to say that they were the destroyers of royal autocracy and of the hereditary divine right of kings; but beyond this they did not secure freedom, nor in the case of the Church did they at all desire to allow it.

On January 3rd, 1645, the day of Laud's attainder, the Long Parliament by an Ordinance took away the Book of Common Prayer, and established in its place the Directory, a manual of directions for the meagre framework of Puritan worship.

On August 23rd, another Ordinance forbade the use of the Prayer Book, in any 'public place of worship or in any private place or family', and fixed a penalty of five pounds for the first offence, ten for the second, and for the third 'one whole year's imprisonment without bail or mainprize'.

SUMMARY OF EVENTS

1603. MARCH. Accession of James I.
1604. JANUARY. Hampton Court Conference.
    FEBRUARY. **The Fourth Prayer Book.**
1603–4. The Canons of 1604.
1604. King James appoints the divines to revise the English Bible.

1607. The six committees of divines begin their work.

1611. **Authorized Version of the Bible.**

1634–60. Destruction of Church ornaments, including stained-glass. windows.

1637. **Scottish Prayer Book** rejected.

1640. Canons of 1640.

The Long Parliament meets.

1645. JANUARY 3RD. The Prayer Book abolished by an Ordinance and the Directory established.

JANUARY 10TH. Execution of Laud.

AUGUST 23RD. Use of the Prayer Book even in private made a penal offence.

1649. JANUARY 30TH. Execution of King Charles I.

1660. Restoration of Church and King, of Parliamentary Government, and of the Prayer Book.

CHAPTER XII

THE SAVOY CONFERENCE

ENGLAND turned with shouts of joy from the rancour and violence of the Commonwealth, from the spiritual despotism of the Presbyterians and of the Independents who ousted them, and from the resulting distraction and impiety, to the Restoration of Church and King, and of Parliamentary institutions. The year 1660 brought freedom of conscience to Churchmen—though, alas! they soon proceeded to revenge themselves by denying it to Nonconformists. So great was the demand for Prayer Books that, before 1660 had reached its close, five editions of the old Book were printed.

But the Prayer Book had not been revised since 1604, and many agreed at least in this—that a new revision was needed. It was the only point about which the two parties in the State did agree, as the Savoy Conference was soon to show. But first, while King Charles II was still in Holland, a company of Presbyterian divines went to The Hague with the Parliamentary deputation that was to bring Charles back (May 10th, 1660), and asked that, as the Prayer Book had long been discontinued, the King should not use it when he landed. They also asked that his chaplains should give up using the surplice. The King replied with his usual keenness of wit, that he would not be restrained himself when others had so much indulgence. But after he was come back the Puritans continued their pressure, and asked that the Prayer Book might be made like the liturgies of the Reformed Churches.

There were nine Bishops still alive; and they made the discreet reply that 'the nearer both their forms and ours come to the liturgy of the ancient Greek and Latin Churches, the less are they liable to the objections of the common enemy'. The King issued a declaration on October 25th, 1660, promising a conference, and allowing freedom meanwhile.

On April 15th, 1661, the Savoy Conference met: it consisted of twelve Bishops (including John Cosin of Durham, Robert Sanderson of Lincoln, and Gilbert Sheldon of London), with nine coadjutors (including John Pearson, author of the famous *Exposition of the Creed*, afterwards Bishop of Chester), Peter Heylin, Peter Gunning, Anthony Sparrow, Herbert Thorndike, on the one side; and on the other, twelve Presbyterian Divines (including Richard Baxter, author of

35. BISHOP COSIN

The Saints' Rest, and Edmund Calamy), with nine coadjutors.

We have not space here to reprint the 'Exceptions' of the Ministers to the Book of Common Prayer, or the 'Answer of the Bishops to the Exceptions': they are given in E. Cardwell's *History of Conferences*. But they throw so valuable a light upon the great battle of the Prayer Book in the 17th century, upon its principles and those of its opponents, that the reader will be glad to have some of the more important Exceptions before him, with the Answers of the Bishops, which here are condensed and printed in italics.

One point emerges at once—the truth of Milton's epigram that Presbyter was but old Priest writ large. Some of the 'Exceptions' are clerical autocracy writ very large indeed: the Puritans wished to give the minister power to refuse Baptism to a child, if he considered its parents to be heretical or notorious sinners. We may be thankful that the Bishops replied, *We think this to be very hard and uncharitable, and giving also too great and arbitrary a power*. Similarly they wished to give greater liberty to the minister in the Absolution (Visitation of the Sick), and the Bishops answered that the giving of absolution must not depend upon *the minister's pleasure*, but on the sick man's penitence. They also desired that the minister should be urged to use full power 'both to admit and to keep from the Lord's Table'. They further proposed to deprive the people of their share in the service—the repetitions and responses, the Kyries after the Commandments (the minister to say instead 'a suitable prayer' at the end), and the alternate reading of the Psalms and Hymns, declaring 'the people's part in public prayer to be only with silence and reverence to attend thereunto, and to declare their consent in the close, by saying *Amen*'. It is not, therefore, to be wondered at that they desired the minister to face the people all through the service: to this the Bishops replied, *Not so*, and pointed out that in the ancient Church the minister always turned *with* the people when he acted as their spokesman.

The minister, thus exalted, must have the entire service in his own hands: the Puritan Divines, therefore, not only wished him to have discretion to 'omit part' of the appointed service and substitute extempore prayer, but also they desired that the collects should be melted down into 'one methodical and entire form of prayer composed out of many of them', and that the

Litany should be changed 'into one solemn prayer'. Think of it—think that if the Bishops had given way in 1661, we should to-day go to church and find a black-coated gentleman con-

36. 'FORASMUCH AS THIS RUBRIC SEEMETH TO BRING BACK'
The Communion, c. 1500.

fronting us to say the whole Litany without a break as one solemn prayer, while we had no share but 'with silence and reverence to attend thereunto' and to say 'Amen' when he had finished!

The Ornaments Rubric was to be omitted, 'forasmuch as this rubric seemeth to bring back the cope, albe, etc., and other vestments forbidden by the Common Prayer Book, 5 and 6 Edw. VI' (the Second Book); to which the Bishops replied, *We think it fit that the rubric continue as it is.* The Surplice, the Cross in Baptism, and kneeling at Communion are objected to as 'fountains of evil'; the wedding-ring is to be optional. There is to be 'nothing in the Liturgy which may seem to countenance the observation of Lent as a religious fast'; and the 'religious observation of saints' days . . . and the vigils thereof is to be omitted'. The word 'Sunday' was objected to, and not only 'Priest', but even that most harmless of words, 'Curate'. The Bishops replied to such criticisms as these by referring to *Catholic usage*, and to *a Custom of the Churches of God, agreeable to the Scripture and ancient*, and to *the Catholic consent of antiquity*.

The Puritan Divines also objected to those phrases in the Prayer Book which assume all the congregation 'to be regenerated, converted, and in an actual state of grace'; the Bishops replied by pointing to St. Paul's use of the word *saints.* The Puritans objected also to the optimistic assumptions of the Burial Service (*It is better to be charitable and hope the best*, said the Bishops), and asked for a rubric declaring that the prayers and exhortations are not for the benefit of the dead (the Bishops significantly ignored this). They also demanded a rubric allowing ministers not to go to the graveside unless they thought fit, to which the Bishop replied that, since this was not asked *for the ease of tender consciences, but of tender heads*, the desire *may be helped by a cap better than a rubric*. Bishops, indeed, were not afraid to be witty in those days, or to speak in homely fashion, as when they met the demand for omitting all Lessons from the Apocrypha by the remark, *It is heartily to be wished that sermons were as good*; for, said they, if nothing ought to be heard in church except the Old and New Testaments, then there would be no sermons either.

Very few at the present day, whether Churchmen or not, would agree with these objections, many of which were undeniably fractious and captious while others depended upon a theology now obsolete. It is a mercy, for instance, that the Bishops did not give way to the Puritan demand that 'inheritors' in the Catechism should be altered to 'heirs'—thus making the Kingdom of Heaven a future hope instead of a present inheritance; and we may be glad the Bishops left the definition of a Sacrament broad, by refusing to put 'Two only', without qualification, though that qualification does now need rewording; for though the Medieval idea that there are exactly seven is a mistake, it would have been a pity to deny that marriage, for instance, is a sacrament. I think we may also be devoutly thankful that we are not fettered to-day by the insertion into the Catechism of the theories current in 1661 'concerning the nature of faith, repentance, the two covenants, justification, sanctification, adoption, and regeneration'.

Who, again, would now desire that Confirmation should not be administered by the Bishop, or that it should not be assumed in that service that the children brought have the Christian spirit and the forgiveness of their sins? Who would now desire to omit the mention of godparents at Baptism or Confirmation? Who would like the minister to have power, if he chose, not to deliver the Sacrament to each communicant individually? Who could bear to see the simple ornaments and ceremonies already mentioned—the surplice, for instance, or the giving of a wedding-ring—abolished?

Of course some of the Puritan criticisms were good, and some were accepted by the Bishops and their coadjutors. They agreed to print the Epistles and Gospels according to the Authorized Version; to add to the rubric 'The portion of Scripture appointed for the Epistle'; to give a longer time for notice by the communicants, altering 'over night, or else in the morning' to 'at least some time the day before'; to add the manual acts to the Consecration in the Communion Service (the Puritans had rightly pointed out that the breaking of the bread was not so much as mentioned); to add (and this was also an improvement) to the rubric after Confirmation the words 'or be ready and desirous to be confirmed'. Besides these things, they agreed to alter in the Marriage Service 'with my body I thee worship' to 'with my body I thee honour', though fortunately this was not done; but they did alter 'till death us depart' to 'till death us do part'. The Bishops further agreed to add the preface ('prefixed by God himself', the Puritans had said) to the Commandments, but fortunately this also was not done; and to omit from the Burial Service the epithets 'in *sure and certain* hope of Resurrection to eternal life'; but very mercifully this was taken back also, the sense being guarded by the insertion of the definite article.

We may summarize the position by two quotations.

The Puritan Divines said:

'To load our public forms with the private fancies upon which we differ, is the most sovereign way to perpetuate schism to the world's end. Prayer, confession, thanksgiving, reading of the Scriptures, and administration of the Sacraments in the plainest, and simplest manner, were matter enough to furnish out a sufficient Liturgy, though nothing either of private opinion, or of church pomp, of garments, or prescribed gestures, of imagery, of musick, of matter concerning the dead, of many superfluities which creep into the Church under the name of *order* and *decency*, did interpose itself. To charge Churches and Liturgies with things unnecessary, was the first beginning of all superstition.' 'If the special guides and fathers of the Church would be a little sparing of encumbering churches with superfluities, or not over-rigid, either in reviving obsolete customs, or imposing new, there would be far less cause of schism, or superstition.'

37. THE CHAPEL OF EDWARD THE CONFESSOR
Westminster Abbey

The shrine is of Cosmati work, dating from 1268 (Henry III). On this is the arcaded wooden canopy of *c.* 1556.

The Bishops and their coadjutors said:

'It was the wisdom of our Reformers to draw up such a Liturgy as neither Romanist nor Protestant could justly except against.' 'For preserving of the Churches' peace we know no better nor more efficacious way than our set Liturgy; there being no such way to keep us from schism, as to speak all the same thing, according to the Apostle. This experience of former and latter times hath taught us; when the Liturgy was duly observed we lived in peace; since that was laid aside there hath been as many modes and fashions of public worship as fancies.' 'If we do not observe that golden rule of the venerable Council of Nice, "Let ancient customs prevail," till reason plainly requires the contrary, we shall give offence to sober Christians by a causeless departure from Catholic usage, and a greater advantage to enemies of our Church, than our brethren, I hope, would willingly grant.'

In many things the Churchmen of that age were in the wrong —the doctrine, for instance, of the divine right of kings still pervaded much Church opinion. But few scholars would now refuse to admit that their theology was broader, more Christian, because less tainted by Calvinism, and truer to the New Testament than that of their opponents; and in those liturgical matters with which this history is concerned there is now little doubt that they were right and the Puritans wrong. Puritanism brought to England a noble stock of moral sturdiness; and the ecclesiastical descendants of those Dissenters whom the cruelty of the Clarendon Code put outside the pale of the law, are among the best of our people to-day; but those very descendants are themselves the surest witnesses to-day that the Churchmen were right, on the whole, in liturgical matters; for our modern Presbyterians and Free Churchmen are steadily adopting the very phrases and customs and ornaments to which the saintly Richard Baxter and his colleagues so strongly objected.

After the Savoy Conference the last English revision of the Prayer Book was put in hand, and our present Book of Common Prayer—the Fifth English Prayer Book—was produced. Like the Fourth Book, it had the sanction of Convocation—a more formal and thorough sanction than any of its predecessors. We shall express this most briefly and clearly by a summary of these important events:

SUMMARY OF EVENTS

1645. Prayer Book abolished and its use made penal.

1660. The Restoration.

MAY 1ST. King Charles II issues the Declaration of Breda promising toleration.

MAY 4TH. Parliamentary Deputation of Presbyterians to the King at The Hague.

MAY 10TH. Prayer Book of 1604 used before the Lords on Thanksgiving Day.

OCT. 25TH. Royal Declaration promising a Conference and the decision of 'a national Synod'.

1661. APRIL 15TH–JULY 24TH. The Savoy Conference.

MAY 8TH. Convocation meets.

JULY 9TH. Commons pass Bill of Uniformity.

NOV. 20TH. Convocation appoints a Committee of Bishops to revise the Prayer Book.

DEC. 20TH. **Fifth Prayer Book** completed, after discussion and amendment, and adopted by both houses of the Convocations of Canterbury and York.

1662. FEB. 25TH. Fifth Prayer Book annexed to the Bill of Uniformity, but without discussion or amendment in either house.

APRIL 9TH. Lords pass Bill of Uniformity.

MAY 19TH. The Bill receives the royal assent and becomes the Act of Uniformity of 1662.

It has been sometimes said as a gibe against the Prayer Book that it is part of an Act of Parliament. So it is, and so are the Lord's Prayer and the Psalms of David, and so might anything be. The above summary shows that, though Parliament chose to adopt the Church's Prayer Book (which was an honour to both parties), to annex it to an Act of Uniformity, thus giving it civil sanction, and (most regrettably) to enforce it with pains and penalties, our present Prayer Book was not one whit less the work of the Church, whose rights and liberties were carefully safeguarded at every stage. The troublous century which we call the Reformation Period began amid violence and oppression, but it ended with the establishment of constitutionalism in 1662; and the royalist Parliament which enforced the settlement did at least represent the people.

The more then is it to be regretted that this Parliament refused the promised toleration to the Puritans, who now from being Nonconformist Churchmen became Dissenters, their worship forbidden by the Conventicle Act of 1664 under a final penalty of transportation, their extremer ministers refused permission to come within five miles of a town by the Five Mile Act of 1665, and their conscientious members debarred, in common with Papists, from all civil, military, and naval office by the Test Act of 1673. There was, however, some excuse for a Parliament composed mainly of country squires, who had many of them come back to their native villages at the Restoration, to find the church smashed, the trees felled, and the home of their ancestors destroyed. The Puritan ministers also, who were ejected, were, after all, themselves intruders; for there had been a worse ejectment of Anglicans before. Above all this, there loomed in men's minds the indelible memory of 'King Charles the Martyr'.

CHAPTER XIII

THE FIFTH ENGLISH PRAYER BOOK

THE Savoy Conference came to an end in July, 1661: before the Christmas of that year Convocation had completed the Fifth Prayer Book, which is the book still used in England to-day; and the next year this was annexed to the Act of Uniformity. The preceding chapter has, we hope, shown the conditions under which the new Prayer Book was produced and the principles which actuated the revisers. These are stated with much clearness in the first of the present prefaces to the English Prayer Book, which was then added, and is called simply *The Preface.*

'The Preface' was written by Sanderson, Bishop of Lincoln, and is divided into five paragraphs: 1. A description of the previous revisions: in the often misquoted phrase, they had been intended 'to keep the mean between the two extremes, *of too much stiffness in refusing, and of too much easiness in admitting any variation*'. 2. A sketch of those preliminaries to the present revision (the deputation to the king, &c.) which were described in our last chapter. The harsh tone of a triumphant party will be noticed in the Bishop's phrases. 3. The standard by which proposed changes were accepted or rejected, with a proviso that the Book of 1604 contained nothing contrary to the Word of God. Here is another famous and important sentence: 'We have rejected all such as were either of dangerous consequence (as secretly striking at some established doctrine, or laudable practice of the Church of England, or indeed of the whole Catholick Church of Christ) or else of no consequence at all, but utterly frivolous and vain.' 4. A description of the changes introduced, beginning with a statement that they were not made 'to gratify this or that party in any their unreasonable demands'. 5. An expression of the hope that these changes (though unwelcome to 'men of factious, peevish, and perverse spirits') will be approved by 'all sober, peaceable, and truly conscientious sons of the Church of England'.

Vera Effigies Reverendi in Christo Patris Dñi:
ROBERTI SANDSERSON
EPISCOPI LINCOLNIENSIS.

38. BISHOP SANDERSON

THE PRINCIPAL CHANGES

The changes described in this Preface are—1. (DIRECTIONS) the better direction of the officiant, 2. (VERBAL) the alteration of obsolete phrases, 3. (SCRIPTURE) the use of the Authorized Version, especially for the Epistles and Gospels,

4. (ADDITIONS) some new prayers and thanksgivings, especially for use at Sea, and an order for the Baptism of Adults.

These alterations are about 600 in number. Let us endeavour to summarize the more important under the four heads just mentioned.

1. DIRECTIONS.

Mattins and Evensong. The Five Prayers (including the 'state prayers') which had previously been appended to the Litany, were added to the Divine Service. They had been better left where they were; but this was a time of strong royalist reaction. The rubric concerning them also mentions the Anthem, 'in Quires and Places where they sing'; the Anthem had not been mentioned in the earlier Prayer Books, but the Elizabethan Injunctions of 1559 had authorized 'an hymn or such like song' at this place, which was then the end of the service.

Holy Communion. After the Creed the old rubric had merely ordered a Sermon or Homily, and then (*after* the Sermon) the curate was to give notice of Holy-days and Fasting-days, to exhort the people to remember the poor, and to read one or more of the sentences. The rubrics which we now have were taken from the Scottish Liturgy of 1637, as was the rubric after the sentences, ordering the priest to place the Bread and Wine on the Table.

The rubric before the Consecration ('When the Priest, standing before the Table, hath so ordered', &c.) was added, and also the direction for the Fraction and other manual acts, heretofore left to tradition. The very questionable rubric providing for a second consecration by the mere repetition of the so-called Words of Institution was reinserted. The two rubrics were added ordering that what remains of the Sacrament after the Communion shall be covered with a linen veil, and afterwards reverently consumed.

Confirmation. The first part of the rubric 'To the end that Confirmation', &c., was made into the Preface. The Catechism (with which the Order of Confirmation had begun) was now printed separately; and in its stead was inserted the Bishop's question—'Do ye here . . . renew the solemn promise', &c.

Marriage. A form was added for publishing Banns. The rubric after the Blessing 'Then shall begin the Communion' was omitted, and the concluding direction that the new-married persons 'must' receive the Communion was altered. *Visitation of the Sick.* The words 'Here shall the sick person be moved to make a special Confession of his sins, if', &c., were substituted for 'Here shall the sick person make a special confession, if', &c.; and the words 'if he humbly and heartily desire it' were added. The rubrics also for the Communion were made clearer. *Burial.* The rubric about the excommunicate, &c., was added. Psalms 116 and 139 had been given in the First Book, but since the Second Book there had been none: now Psalms 39 and 90 were given—but the selection might have been better. The Lesson instead of being said at the graveside was wisely ordered to be read in Church. The name of the departed person was omitted from the prayer, 'Almighty God, with whom'. *Churching.* Psalms 116 and 127 were substituted for Psalm 121. The *Commination* was ordered to be used on Ash Wednesday.

2. VERBAL ALTERATIONS.

The more important were: In Divine Service and in the Liturgy, 'priest' was substituted for 'minister' at the Absolution. In the *Litany* the words 'rebellion' and 'schism' were significantly added in the Deprecations; and in the Intercessions, 'Bishops, pastors, and ministers' was altered to 'Bishops, Priests, and Deacons'. In several places the word 'congregation' was changed to 'church'. 'Forsake' was well changed to 'renounce' in the Baptismal Vow. In the Ordinal, Cosin's translation of the *Veni Creator*, 'Come, Holy Ghost, our souls inspire', was added.

3. SCRIPTURE.

The *Epistles and Gospels* were taken from the Authorized Version of 1611 (the Gospels for the Sunday after Christmas, Palm Sunday, and Good Friday being shortened, the first by the omission of the Genealogy). The Easter Day Anthems were also enlarged, 'Christ our Passover' and the *Gloria* being added. But the *Psalter* was left in the words of the Great Bible of 1540, which were endeared to the people; the Decalogue also was left; and the Offertory Sentences and Comfortable Words, which are an independent version, were left unaltered.

4. ADDITIONS.

Excellent additions were made in the *Prayers and Thanksgivings*—the two Ember Prayers, the Prayer for Parliament, the Prayer for All Conditions, the General Thanksgiving, and the Thanksgiving for Public Peace. With the exception of the last, which was topical, these are among the best known and loved of all our prayers.

Three *Collects* were changed, and a Collect, Epistle, and Gospel added for Epiphany 6, giving us four of the very finest collects in the book—those for Advent 3, St. Stephen, Epiphany 6, and Easter Even. The Epistle for the Purification was added. In the *Communion Service*, two additions were made to the Church Militant Prayer. To 'accept our alms' was added 'and oblations'; and the commemoration of the departed, 'And we also bless thy holy Name', &c., was put in at the end. The Black Rubric (pasted into the Second Book, 1552, and removed in 1559) was inserted after the service, but with 'real and essential presence' altered to 'corporal presence'.

The service for the *Baptism of Adults* (a less successful effort) was added, as 'The Preface' explains, owing to 'the growth of Anabaptism', and also to the newly felt need of 'the baptizing of natives in our plantations, and others converted to the faith'. Here, then, we have the first sign of the revival of the missionary spirit—though mainly in the 'plantations', that is the colonies—after a lapse of about eight centuries, during which very little had been done. To all the Baptismal Services was added the Vow of Obedience, 'Wilt thou then obediently keep', &c.; and thus they were brought into line with the Catechism.

·39. DR. PETER GUNNING
The author of the Prayer for all Conditions of Men.
He was afterwards Bishop of Ely, as in this portrait.

To the *Visitation of the Sick* (which might have been more radically improved) the Commendation, 'Unto God's gracious mercy', &c., was added; and also the four concluding Occasional Prayers, beautiful but overweighted. The *Forms of Prayer to be used at Sea* were added: these too are overweighted, and are less beautiful.

The Ordinal. The reader will have noticed that few concessions were made to the Puritans, but that on the contrary many things distasteful to them were inserted. In the most significant place of all, the Ordinal, this is specially apparent. In the old form for the Consecration of a Bishop, 'Take the Holy Ghost, and remember that thou stir up', &c., were inserted the words 'for the Office and Work of a Bishop in the Church of God', so as to make it unmistakably clear to the public that a Bishop's office is other than that of a Presbyter. Similarly in the Ordering of Priests, before the words 'Whose sins', &c., was added 'for the Office and Work of a Priest in the Church of God, now committed unto thee by the Imposition of our hands'. The old

40. FRONTISPIECE OF CROUCH'S *Divine Banquet*, 1696.

Showing priest, communicants, and altar of the period.

forms were perfectly good and had ancient precedent; but the additions were made in order to avoid misunderstanding.

It should be mentioned here that in 1662 two more State Services were drawn up by Convocation, those for King Charles the Martyr and for the Restoration, and were added to the Accession Service (Elizabeth's had been made in 1576, and Charles I's in 1626), and to that for Gunpowder Treason, which was altered. These State Services were then annexed to the Prayer Book by the sanction of the Crown and Convocation, and were subsequently enjoined by Royal Proclamation at the beginning of each reign. In 1859, on the petition of Convocation and Parliament, three were revoked, the Accession Service remaining. This last was revised in 1901 and again in 1910; and on June 23rd, 1910, the new form was ordered by Royal Proclamation to be annexed to the Book of Common Prayer and used yearly on the 6th of May. The fine Prayer for Unity was, till these last revisions, the latest composition within the covers of the Prayer Book, having been added at the accession of George I.

The State Services of 1662 are largely modelled upon that for 'Powder Treason', which in its turn reflects the verbose Elizabethan type of special service; and they illustrate the bad side of the period. The prayers indeed have the magnificence of their age, and are full of fine passages; but they are not constructed on sound liturgical lines, and as a consequence will not bear comparison with the prayers of the Prayer Book itself for beauty, conciseness, or simplicity. They are also full of political opinion, their loyalty is expressed in extravagant terms, and they confide to Almighty God their denunciations of 'violent and bloodthirsty men', 'bloody enemies', 'sons of Belial, as on this day, to imbrue their hands in the blood of thine Anointed', 'the unnatural Rebellion, Usurpation, and Tyranny of ungodly and cruel men'—using for preference four words where one would have been too much.

This is magnificent, but it is not peace. Now, when we

remember that these State Services (with additions in subsequent reigns) were cheerfully used throughout the country for nearly two centuries, we can understand one reason for the existence of what came to be called Dissent. As Professor A. F. Pollard says, 'While the State grew more comprehensive, the Church grew more exclusive. It was not that, after 1662, it narrowed formulas or doctrines; but it failed to enlarge them.'

THE EIGHTEENTH CENTURY

The 18th century produced indeed after 1738 the Methodist Revival, a Church of England movement, which has had a greater influence than any other religious movement during the last three or four centuries; it was not an age of religious decadence, but one of much quiet strength, with a clergy far more learned and influential than now, with churches so full that galleries were erected all over the country to hold the overflowing congregations; for nearly every one went to church on Sunday, and it has been computed that only 5 per cent. of the population in the time of Queen Anne belonged to denominations outside the Church of England. The 18th century is often justly reproached with the infrequency of Communion Services; yet it was an age when nearly all Englishmen were communicants, whereas at the present day the proportion has sunk to about 7 or 8 per cent. It was also the century which began with the foundation of missionary work (dormant in Britain since the 9th century) by the S.P.C.K. and the S.P.G., and ended with the humanitarian movement of the Evangelicals for the freeing of the slave. But while we recognize this, and remember the universal acceptance of Christianity, the quiet strong religion of towns and villages, the many saintly parish priests, the abundant prominence of clergy in the Universities and the Royal Society, the influence of scholars like Bishops Berkeley and Butler, and Dr. Johnson, we must also admit the defect of organizing power. It is just this that a history of the Prayer Book most prominently reveals. Nothing was done to bring the missionary and social and intellectual movements into the common prayer of the Church; and the Methodist revival itself gradually found its expression more and more outside the Anglican fellowship. Acts of comprehension, too, would have been possible in many directions, had the dominant Whig authorities been alive to the need; but, until the alteration in 1865 of the form of clerical subscription to the Articles, almost nothing was done during the two centuries and a half which followed the Restoration. It was only in the newly constituted Church of the United States, after the Revolution of 1776, that the Prayer Book was revised.

41. 'A CLERGY FAR MORE LEARNED'

Portrait in wax of Dr. William Adams, Master of Pembroke College, Oxford, and the friend of Dr. Johnson. By Isaac Gosset the Elder, 1784. Dr. Adams wears the ordinary outdoor dress of the clergy in the 17th and 18th centuries, gown and tippet (scarf) over his cassock, with the clerical wig of the period.

In the possession of Sir Francis Adams Hyett, Painswick.

HYMNS

The spread of hymnody would have counteracted the liturgical stagnation; but the parish churches went on using the two official metrical psalters, the *Old Version* and the *New Version* throughout the 18th century; so that the effect of the new hymn-books was to draw people away from the Church of England.

English hymnody had begun—even before the First Prayer

Book, with the *Old Version*—as it came to be called—of Metrical Psalms (Sternhold, 1548 and 1549; Sternhold and Hopkins, 1551, 1559, and 1561; Day's Complete Psalter, 1562).

The *Old Version*, 'The Whole Booke of Psalmes', known as 'Sternhold and Hopkins', contains, after the Psalms, paraphrases of the *Veni Creator*, *Venite*, *Te Deum*, *Benedicite*, *Benedictus*, *Magnificat*, *Nunc Dimittis*, Athanasian Creed, Ten Commandments, Lord's Prayer; and also ten hymns, one of which is to be sung before the Sermon, one is a 'Thanksgiving after receiving of the Lord's Supper', one 'to be sung before Morning Prayer,' and one before Evening Prayer. Of these hymns and paraphrases 'O Lord, turn not away thy face' is the only survivor to-day. From the

42. INTERIOR OF ST. MARY'S, LICHFIELD, *c.* 1760

Dr. Johnson was baptized in this English Renaissance church in 1709, and regularly attended it when in his native town till his last year, 1784. The parson is conducting the service from the desk beneath the pulpit. He wears surplice and bands. The emphasis of the period is on the intellectual rather than the aesthetic aspects of religion; but none the less the altar here is typically dignified in its simplicity. The galleries made room for the large numbers that were anxious to hear the prayers and the sermon.

Psalms we retain the famous version of Psalm 100, the 'Old Hundredth'—'All people that on earth doe dwell'.

The old Sternhold and Hopkins continued to be used in the majority of churches right through the 18th century, but in London and other centres it gave place to the *New Version* of Tate and Brady ('allowed by the King in Council', 1696), with its new *Supplement*. The *Supplement* in its earliest known edition (1700) includes 'While shepherds watched', as well as paraphrases of the Canticles, Lord's Prayer, &c., and five now forgotten hymns, two for Easter and three for the Communion. The third edition is dated 1702. The sixth edition, 1708, added to these 'O Lord, turn not thy face from me' and two others. In 1782 'Hark! the herald angels sing', 'My God, and is thy table spread', 'Awake, my soul, and with the sun', and two others, now forgotten, were added. On some date after 1807 the Easter Hymn ('Jesus Christ is risen to-day') and 'Glory to thee, my God, this night' were further added.

Hymnody indeed developed greatly in the 18th century, through the prolific genius of Isaac Watts and Charles Wesley in especial. Of Watts's hymns over 600 were found, by that careful hymnologist, James Mearns, to have been still printed in books issued since 1860; while Charles Wesley wrote at least 6,500 hymns, the complete edition of them occupying thirteen octavo volumes. But throughout the century the parish churches were content with the old Metrical Psalters.

With the 19th century, however, came a torrent of Church of England hymn-books, reaching its first height between 1820 and 1840, when over sixty books were published. Ten of these were issued in one year, 1833, and forty between 1830 and 1840. In the decade between 1850 and 1860 there appeared forty-three hymnals, the best known being the *Hymnal Noted* (1852 and 1854), Murray's *Hymnal* (1852), Cooke and Denton's *Church Hymnal* (1853), and Mercer's *Church Psalter and Hymn Book* (1854). At the end of this decade, when Mercer's collection was taking the lead, a syndicate was formed of several copyright holders who agreed to withdraw their books in favour of a new venture (Neale's

THE PSALMES OF David
in Meetre.

Beatus vir. PSAL. I. T. S.

The Pſalme is ſet forſt as a preface to exhort all godly men to vertue and meditate the heauenly wiſedome: for they be blesſed that ſo doe; but the wicked contemnes thereof, at length ſhall come to miſery.

He man is blest that hath

not bent to wicked rede his eare: nor led

his life as ſinners doe, nor ſate in ſcorners

chaire, 2. But in the law of God the

Lord, doth ſet his whole delight : And

in that law doth exerciſe himſelfe both

day and night.

3 He ſhall be like the tree that groweth,
faſt by the waters ſide:
Which bringeth forth moſt pleaſant fruit,
in her due time and tide.
Whoſe leaſe ſhall neuer fade nor fall,
but flouriſh ſtill and ſtand:
Euen ſo all things ſhall proſper well,
that this man takes in hand.

4 So ſhall not the vngodly men,
they ſhall be nothing ſo:
But as the duſt which from the earth,
the wind driues to and fro.
5 Therefore ſhall not the wicked men
in iudgement ſtand vpright:
Nor yet the ſinners with the iuſt,
ſhall come in place or ſight.

6 For why? the way of godly men,
vnto the Lord is knowne:
And eke the way of wicked men,
ſhall quite be ouerthrowne.

Quare fremuerunt, Pſal. II. T. S.

and of the worlde. Therefore he exhorteth Princes humbly to ſubmit themſelues vnder the ſame. Herein is ſignified Chriſt and his kingdome.

Sing this as the firſt Pſalme.

WHy did the Gentiles tumults raiſe
what rage was in their brain?
Why did the Iewiſh people muſe,
ſeeing all is but vaine.
2 The Kinges and Rulers of the earth,
conſpire and are all bent:
Againſt the Lord, and Chriſt his ſonne,
which he amongſt vs ſent.

3 Shall we be bound to them ſay they
let all their bonds be broke:
And of their doctrine and their law,
let vs reiect the yoke.
4 But he that in the heauen dwelleth,
their doinges will deride:
And make them all as mocking ſtocks,
throughout the world ſo wide.

5 For in his wrath the Lord will ſay,
to them vpon a day:
And in his fury trouble them,
and then the Lord will ſay.
6 I haue annointed him my King,
vpon my holy hill:
I will therefore Lord preach thy law,
and eke declare thy will.

7 For in this wiſe the Lord himſelfe
did ſay to me I wot:
Thou art my deare and onely ſonne,
to day I thee begot.
8 All people I will giue to thee,
as heires at thy requeſt:
The ends and coaſts of all the earth,
by thee ſhall be poſſeſt.

9 Thou ſhalt them bruſe euen with a mace,
as men vnder foote trode:
And as the potters ſheardes ſhalt breake
them with an iron rod.
10 Now ye O Kings and Rulers all,
be wiſe therefore and learnd:
By whom the matters of the world,
be iudged and diſcernd.

11 See that yee ſerue the Lord aboue,
in trembling and in feare:
See that with reuerence ye reioice,
to him in like manner.
12 See that ye kiſſe and eke embrace,
his bleſſed ſonne I ſay:
Leſt in his wrath yee ſodainely,
periſh in the midway.

13 If once his wrath neuer ſo ſmall,
ſhall kindle in his breaſt
O h then all they that truſt in Chriſt,

A 2   ſhall

---

43. 'STERNHOLD AND HOPKINS.' THE OLD VERSION OF METRICAL PSALMS

From a copy, 1607, bound up with a James I Prayer Book and a Geneva Bible.

all-important work in the *Hymnal Noted* being at his own wish free for any one to appropriate without question of copyright): thus provided, the syndicate printed in 1859 a trial copy, called *Hymns*, and this in 1861 became the first edition of *Hymns Ancient and Modern*, which contained 273 hymns, of which 12 only were original and 33 were from Neale: it was in vain that his friends protested, and compared the forty members of the committee with the eponymous heroes of Ali Baba's story; Neale had presented his work to the Church, other rivals had been brought in, many of the clergy had pledged themselves to adopt the new book; and above all the title, cumbrous as it now seems, exactly hit the mood of an age which had just built the Albert Memorial and was yearning for things ancient and crocketed. As a matter of fact there were fewer English hymns than Latin in the collection—131 to 132; but Chandler (in his *Hymns of the Primitive Church*, 1837) and others made the mistake of thinking everything ancient that was in Latin: the original of 'On Jordan's bank', for instance, like others by Coffin, is later than Isaac Watts; and Julian points out in his *Dictionary of Hymnology* that about one-half of the Latin hymns in *Ancient and Modern* were not as old as Sternhold and Hopkins. He attributes the huge success of the book to the causes we have mentioned, although he considers 'its text the most mutilated in the Church', its literary standard not a good one, and its range of subjects 'very limited'.

Julian indeed places on a higher level those later hymnals which appeared in the following twenty years, the *Hymnal Companion* (1870), *Church Hymns* (1871), and Thring's *Church of England Hymn-book* (1880), the last of which he ranks before all the others, though indeed its long title must have militated against a popular success. During the present century, however, the atmosphere has completely changed; and to us these books all 'date' and seem but slight modifications of the pattern—

with too much of what an irreverent critic has recently called
'the crinoline hymn and the chignon tune'. The really fine,
original, and enduring hymns at this time were written by
Americans—Whittier, Samuel Longfellow, Samuel Johnson,
Hosmer, and others; and these, together with a few by English
poets like Palgrave and (at the close of the century) the Poet
Laureate, Robert Bridges, have in the 20th century come to be
included in our new hymnals. English music, too, which was
at its lowest ebb between 1870 and 1900, recovered at the
beginning of the present century, and is now in the front rank
and second to no other.

We have only to imagine our Sunday services to-day without
hymns, in order to realize how large an element they have become in public worship, and how much they have done already to
save the Church from narrowness, unreality, and impotence. By
great good fortune the English Church, since the disappearance
of Tate and Brady, has been saved from the frozen mediocrity
of an imposed official hymnal; and thus hymnody has grown
in its charitable comprehensiveness, has steadily improved in
words and music, and has won for itself a place deep in the
heart of the people. Hymns have broken many fetters, and can
keep a Church abreast of the age.

PRAYER BOOK REVISION

Prayer Book revision in America will be dealt with in the
next chapter. In England since 1662 less has been accomplished.
There was an impracticable attempt at revision in the reign of
William III, happily abortive; and additional services, rare in
the Georgian era, have been since increased, especially during
recent years (see p. 41). In 1871 the Lectionary was revised,
and a great opportunity was missed. A further Revised Lectionary was produced for England in 1922; but this Lectionary
is also a grave impediment: many Sunday services are weakened

by the length and shapelessness of the Lessons there provided, when they are read as they stand. A new Lectionary, especially for the Sundays, is still the most urgently needed reform; for

44. THE SEEMLINESS OF THE CHURCH BEFORE THE GOTHIC REVIVAL

A Wedding at St. Margaret's, Westminster, in 1804.

Much used to be said about the slovenly condition of our churches before the days of the Gothic Revival and the Oxford Movement; but this is not borne out by historical evidence. Here is a typical example during the reign of George III. Fashions changed during the Victorian era, but not always for the better. The altar is properly vested and is decked with silver-gilt plate: on it are the two texts richly bound; a chalice can also be seen, and a corporal doubtless covering the elements in preparation for Holy Communion. The priest wears a surplice with bands: a scarf also seems to be suggested. Behind the bride stands the clerk, holding an open book.

modern congregations are very different from those of a hundred years ago. The sermon is in the hands of the clergy themselves, and so is the use of a good hymn book in the place of the inadequate products of the Victorian era; but the provision of

Lessons that can be understood and appreciated must be made by authority. Meanwhile the Book of Homilies of 1623 does give the minister power to modify or change Lessons.

In 1872 the Shortened Services Act was passed in England and received the assent of the Crown, after being duly ratified by the Convocations. It therefore has the authority which the Revision of 1928 failed to secure. Although it does not go very far, it contains many useful provisions which have been little realized because they have been passed over in books about public worship. The Act, for instance, makes it perfectly lawful and canonical for a sermon to be preached at Mattins and Evensong, as well as for hymns to be sung at any point in a service. The Act also allows collects instead of the Bidding Prayer before the Sermon; it gives permission for the Litany to be used after Evening Prayer or instead of it; and a sermon may accompany the Litany.

A very important provision of the Shortened Services Act gives the Ordinary power to dispense with one or more of the prescribed services on Sundays and Holy-days in any church when their use is attended with serious inconvenience. It also allows special services with the approval of the Ordinary, so long as they consist of hymns, anthems, and extracts from the Bible and Prayer Book; but we now go further than that. It also allows (outside cathedral and collegiate churches) a considerable shortening of the week-day services, which may contain only one Psalm, one Canticle, and one Lesson (an excellent system for the purpose), and may be shortened also by the omission of the Exhortation, while the services may conclude after the Creed with the Suffrages, three Collects, the Prayer of St. Chrysostom, and the Grace. These provisions used to be much criticized; but time has justified their principles, and the continuous indiscriminate reading of the entire Psalter and Bible is now desired by few people.

In 1927, after many years of discussion, a new revised Prayer Book, called 'The Deposited Book', was approved by the National Church Assembly by 517 votes to 133. The Measure was passed by the House of Lords, but rejected by a small majority in the House of Commons. The Book was then slightly amended and embodied in a new Measure: the vote in the Church Assembly now sank to 396 in favour of the Book, and it was defeated in the House of Commons by an increased majority of 266 to 220. It therefore did not receive the assent of the Crown, nor was it submitted to the Convocations for final ratification. It has thus no authority and cannot be regarded as a new English Prayer Book: but most bishops have stated that they will not proceed against any incumbent who, with the approval of his Church Council, confines his deviations from the Prayer Book of 1662 to those allowed in the Deposited Book of 1928. Thus in practice the Deposited Book allows a good deal of elasticity under the Ordinary, which is necessary and indeed inevitable; and much experience is accumulating which will be valuable in a future revision. It is very generally felt that, together with a great deal of admirable new material, there is a certain amount that needs alteration, and few perhaps now would wish to see a new Prayer Book for the coming generation laid down in exactly the form of the Deposited Book.

What seemed at first to many a blow to the Church of England, and to the Establishment that has brought so much good both to Church and State, may well prove to have been a blessing in disguise. It was of enormous significance that the Houses of Parliament should have devoted so many days to the discussion of public worship, and 'with such sincerity that cavilling was silenced'; Continental observers were astonished, and it was well said among them, 'We envy you your controversies'. The people of England care about their Church, and are profoundly interested in its ways of worship. Indeed it may be said that the failure of the book was really due to the Bishops having sometimes forgotten the Nation in their pre-occupation with small groups of partisans in the Church.

A Member of Parliament who took a leading part in support-ing the Measure said the last word upon the subject: 'The House of Commons will pass anything that the whole Church wants; but it will pass nothing about which the Church itself is divided.' The statesmanship indeed of the leaders of the Church at that time was in fault: agreement should have been obtained; and matters against which there were substantial majorities in the Assembly (and much larger opposition in the country) should have been dropped.

In America the Prayer Book was revised without controversy because the bishops wisely delegated the work to a commission consisting of bishops, priests, and laymen in equal numbers. In England this was not done: overworked bishops for many years laboured alone, with the result that a master of English like Robert Bridges (who seems to have been created for such a task) had no part in the work, while Dr. Brightman, the most learned liturgical scholar in England, perhaps in the world, publicly expressed his disapproval of the Deposited Book as soon as it was published; and Professor Saintsbury, whose knowledge of literature gave him a supreme position in a criticism, publicly denounced it in *The Times*.

We wait, then, prayerfully and with a good hope, for a future day, a day not very far remote, when the Church shall have emerged from the confusion which the controversies of a hundred years have left behind them, and a new revision will become possible. Such a revision as we need will be not only skilful in its liturgical science, but noble in its art, and worthy of the splendour of our present Bible and Prayer Book; and it will be also Christian in its charitable inclusiveness, not fearing freedom because there is freedom in Nonconformity, nor beauty because there is beauty in the rest of Christendom; so that the Church, no longer encumbered by the armour of obsolete polemics, shall be simple in her teaching as the Gospels are simple, and pure in heart as they are pure.

LAST SUMMARY

1661. DEC. 20TH. Convocation adopts the **Fifth English Prayer Book.**

1662. MAY 19TH. Act of Uniformity. Issue of *Fifth English Prayer Book.*

1689. (William III.) Attempted Revision of the Prayer Book.

1694. Isaac Watts begins writing his hymns. (*Hymns and Spiritual Songs*, printed 1707.)

1696. The '**New Version**' of Metrical Psalms (Tate and Brady), published with authorization of the King in Council.

1700. First Edition of *The Supplement* to the New Version.

1722. The *Liturgy* of 1637 revived in Scotland.

1737. **America:** John Wesley publishes his first hymn book for use in the Church, at Charlestown, Georgia.

1760. Madan's Hymnal, followed by a few others.

1764. **Scottish Liturgy,** the received text.

1786. Bishop Seabury's Communion Service for his diocese of Connecticut.

1789. **The American Prayer Book** (revised in subsequent years, and in 1929).

1801–20. Forty-two new hymnals published.

1833. Ten new hymnals published this year.

1852. J. M. Neale's *Hymnal Noted.*

1861. *Hymns Ancient and Modern.*

1870. Bishop Bickersteth's *Hymnal Companion.*

1871. *Church Hymns.*

1871. English Lectionary revised.

1872. **Shortened Services Act.**

1877. **The Irish Prayer Book.**

1879. England: Attempted Revision, 'The Convocation Prayer Book'.

1881. Revised Version of New Testament.

1884. Revised Version of Old Testament.

1906. *The English Hymnal.*

1901, 1910. Revisions of Accession Service.

1912. **Scottish Prayer Book.** Including the Scottish Liturgy, slightly revised.

1921. **Canadian Prayer Book.**

1922. English Lectionary revised.

1925. *Songs of Praise*, original edition.

1927 and 1928. England: The Deposited Book.

1927. Irish Prayer Book revised.

1929. American Prayer Book revised.

1929. Scottish Prayer Book revised.

1930. Revision completed in South Africa.

1931. *Songs of Praise*, enlarged edition.

CHAPTER XIV

THE PRAYER BOOK IN AMERICA AND IN OTHER CHURCHES OF THE ANGLICAN COMMUNION

THE Prayer Book appeared early in North America. In 1578 Martin Frobisher (who was knighted ten years later for his services against the Spanish Armada) explored what is now a part of Canada, the Hudson's Bay Territory, and for the second time visited 'Frobisher's Bay'. It is on record that on this occasion 'Maister Wolfall', the chaplain, held services and celebrated the Communion. A year later, in 1579, Sir Francis Drake, fighting his way round the world, after sailing through the Straits of Magellan spent six weeks with his party on the shores of California, where the services were conducted by the chaplain, Fletcher. At the place where the first service was held a huge 'Prayer Book Cross' was dedicated in 1892.

In 1583 Sir Humphrey Gilbert took possession of New-foundland, and the first of the laws for the new Colony was that its religion should be 'in public exercise according to the Church of England'. Next year came Sir Walter Ralegh's Colony of Virginia (which Ralegh never visited, the settlement being made by his cousin, Sir Richard Grenville, the hero of the *Revenge*), where Thomas Heriot conducted the Prayer Book services. In Ralegh's second Colony, 'Roanoke' in North Carolina, we have again some evidence; for Manteo, an Indian chieftain, was baptized in 1587, and a week later there was christened the first white baby born in the continent of North America, Virginia Dare; but the first colonies died away, the necessity of some patient unproductive preliminary years not having been yet realized, and the only traces of the first settlers

in North Carolina which later visitors found were some blue-
eyed Red Indians.

In 1606, however, more enduring work was made possible
by the formation of 'regulated' companies of merchants with
a charter from the Crown; and the expedition of the London

45. CHRIST CHURCH, SHREWSBURY, NEW JERSEY
The parish history goes back to 1702, and the Queen Ann communion plate is still in use. The present church was built in
1769, replacing an earlier one of 1738. A meeting was held in
this church, in 1786, Dr. Seabury being present, to consider
the appointment of an episcopate for the Church in America.

Company to Virginia was the true foundation of the United
States of America. In 1607 the first Virginian colony began on
Jamestown Island: on the first Sunday a sail was hung up, and
a bough between two trees served as a pulpit for the first service,
Robert Hunt being the chaplain. The Church of England was
the established or authorized religion of the new State.

The colonization of the northern group of States, New
England, was very different. Its real origin was in 1620, when

the hundred Pilgrim Fathers from Plymouth landed from the *Mayflower* near Cape Cod. These pilgrims were Independents (or Brownists as they were then called) of extreme Puritan views, from Lincolnshire, who had fled to Holland to escape the danger of persecution from the bishops of James I, and by an accident in navigation failed to land in Virginia. They were followed about the year 1629 by some colonists from Dorchester of still more uncompromising views, who founded the State of Massachusetts, where citizenship was made dependent upon membership of a religious congregation, and men were banished and even put to death for their religious opinions. In Connecticut also (a separate colony in 1638), Congregationalism, as we now call it, was the established religion; but both this State and Rhode Island were honourably distinguished for upholding liberty of conscience. Still it was some time before much use was made of the Prayer Book in New England.

When, however, the Revolution severed connexion with the mother country and the Declaration of Independence was signed, July 4th, 1776, there were Church congregations in all the States. But there were no bishops whatever; and there was no representative body. Now that the colonies were independent it was necessary that the Church should be properly organized: a meeting was therefore called in New York at which eight States were represented, and it was agreed to call a general convention for the following year in Philadelphia. Meanwhile the Anglican Church in Connecticut had chosen Dr. Samuel Seabury as the first American Protestant Bishop; he sailed to England, and, failing to obtain consecration there, he went to Scotland where he was duly consecrated by three Scottish bishops, and returned as Bishop of Connecticut in the August of 1785.

The General Convention met next month in Philadelphia, the New England States not being represented: a committee was appointed which issued the 'Proposed Book'; but some of the proposals, which included the omission of the Nicene Creed and the Athanasian Canticle (and the omission of 'He descended into hell'), were too drastic and were rejected in each of the States. Bishop Seabury strongly resisted the Proposed Book,

and urged that revision should be delayed until more bishops had been consecrated. And he took the momentous step, in accordance with a 'concordat' he had made with his Scottish consecrators, of recommending a new Communion Service similar to that of the Scottish Non-Jurors, which was in substance that of Archbishop Laud, as we have already mentioned on p. 97. It is said that Seabury won his

46. SAMUEL SEABURY
FIRST BISHOP OF CONNECTICUT
From an engraving of the portrait by T. S. Duchs, 1786.

hearers to the new Liturgy by his beautiful reading of it.

The English archbishops now helped; and in 1787 Dr. William White was consecrated in Lambeth Chapel as Bishop of Pennsylvania, with Dr. Samuel Provoost as Bishop of New York. A second General Convention met in Philadelphia in 1789, with three bishops, and a house of clerical and lay deputies. As a result, the American Prayer Book was drawn up, in its main lines much as it is to-day. In 1792 the Ordinal was added, and in 1799 the Form for the Consecration of a Church, and in 1804 an Office of Institution of Ministers.

The chief difference is, as we have said, that the American Liturgy follows in the main what we are calling the First Model, that, namely, of the First Prayer Book of 1549, upon which Laud's abortive Scottish Book and the Present Scottish Liturgy have been based. In some ways, however, the American Liturgy follows the Second Model, that of the Second Book, 1552, and of the present English Book, 1662. (The general characteristics of the First Model are described on pp. 58, 218.) We may add here that the omission of the words 'may be unto us the body and blood' wisely avoids a difficulty that was one of the chief causes of the rejection of the English revision of 1928.

All references to English political conditions were of course omitted, and prayers for the President and for Congress were inserted. The Athanasian Canticle was omitted also, and the sign of the cross in Baptism was made optional (with the result that the prejudice against it died out—and a valuable lesson in the wisdom of liberty was learned). There were also verbal alterations, and the form of absolution in the Visitation of the Sick was discarded. Forms for the Visitation of Prisoners, for Thanksgiving for the Fruits of the Earth, as well as for Family Prayer were added. Thanksgiving Day is a purely American Festival; it was in 1789 chosen for the first Thursday in November or for such other day as should be fixed by the Civil Authority. That authority has for long selected the last Thursday in November; and the annual appointment of the day by the President and by the Governors of most of the States is the most notable official recognition of religion in the United States. The Articles were not bound up with the Prayer Book till 1801.

This Book remained in use till 1892, when a Revised Prayer Book was passed by the Convention. It was, however, too conservative; and a Commission was appointed in 1913 to work out a further revision. As a result, the present *Book of Common Prayer according to the Use of the Protestant Episcopal Church of the United States of America* was approved in 1928 and came into use on Advent Sunday 1929.

The Form for Thanksgiving Day, included in the Book of 1892, has been omitted from the present Prayer Book; but the Psalm, Collect, Epistle, and Gospel are included in the appropriate section, and the Thanksgiving, 'Most gracious God by whose knowledge' among the other Thanksgivings. The Form for the Visitation of Prisoners has been replaced by a Prayer in the section of Prayers and Thanksgivings.

The American Book is an excellent one to use. It allows several convenient adaptations and abbreviations, such as the optional omission of 'Dearly Beloved' and the following matter, and of the Decalogue. The last four verses of the *Venite* are rightly omitted (as in the English Deposited Book), and two other verses are added, together with Invitatories. The Litany may very rightly end at the Lord's Prayer; the Marriage Service is shortened.

An American Churchman in England would notice tne absence of these improvements, and also a few verbal differences in the Lord's Prayer ('which' for 'who', 'in earth' for 'on earth', 'them that trespass' for 'those who trespass', and the omission of 'and' before 'the power'), and the *Te Deum* ('honourable' for 'adorable', 'thou didst not abhor the Virgin's womb' for 'thou didst humble thyself to be born of a Virgin'), and the lack of the additional verse to the *Benedicite*, 'Let us bless the Father, and the Son, and the Holy Ghost'. An Englishman in America would notice that the American Book adds new Canticles, *Benedictus es* (Song of the Three Children, the verses preceding the *Benedicite* in the Apocrypha), *Bonum est confiteri* (Ps. 92), and *Benedic, anima mea* (Ps. 103); and there are minor differences of arrangement. Among the Collects, Epistles, and

Gospels provision is made for a second service on Christmas, Easter, and Whitsun Days; also for 'A Saint's Day' (with two

47. INTERIOR OF ST. JAMES'S, GOOSE CREEK
South Carolina
The parish was established in 1705, and this church was built in 1713.

Collects) and a Dedication Festival, and for the Ember and Rogation Days, for Independence Day, Thanksgiving Day, and for a Marriage and a Funeral. The rhythm has been missed in getting rid of the Turks from the Third Good Friday Collect; but the new Collects throughout are simple and strong.

It will be convenient, in mentioning the rich store of new Prayers and Thanksgivings of the American Book, to compare these with those of the Scottish, Irish, and Canadian Books. In addition to some of the old (including the Ember Prayers) in the original Book of 1662 (the present English Book), all four have the following:

American, Scottish, Irish, Canadian

Rogation Prayers.   For Unity.   For Missions.
During Convention,   Confirmation Candi- Social Justice and
   Council or Synod.   dates.   Peace.
The Sick.   Travellers.

Our list must condense a little, since some subjects are provided for by certain Books in other ways, and the titles vary also; but the following are conspicuous:

American, Scottish, Irish

Schools, Colleges, Universities.   Increase of Ministry.

American, Scottish, Canadian

Army and Navy.   Memorial Occasions.

Scottish, Irish, Canadian

New Year.   During Elections.   Hospitals.

In Two Books

Religious Education. Family of Nations.   Absent Friends.
   (*Am., Can.*)   (*Am., Scot.*)   (*Scot., Irish*)

American

Congress.	State Legislature.	Courts of Justice.
Our Country.	The Church.	Children.
Christian Service.	Every Man in his Work.	Prisoners.

Irish

| Christian Citizen-ship. | Ireland. | Local Industries. |
| Sailors. | The Lord's Day. | Recollection. |

And 'A Prayer of the Eastern Church', a general intercession.

In one way and another all these Prayer Books provide also for the bereaved and those in other necessity. In the *Thanksgiving* section, less is added to what was in the English Prayer Book. The American and Scottish Books add one for Harvest; the American and Irish, one for Recovery from Sickness; the American and Canadian, one for a Safe Return; the Scottish and Irish, one for Oversea Missions; and the Irish, one for the Church. In all, the old Thanksgiving for Fair Weather is recast.

The *Bidding Prayer* is printed in the American, Scottish, and Canadian Prayer Books. In England it is only officially printed among the Canons of 1603.

The new *Occasional Services* in all the Books are mentioned in Chapter XVII.

THE SCOTTISH PRAYER BOOK

Laud's Scottish Prayer Book of 1637 did not come into use: the Episcopal services until the Restoration were hardly distinguishable from the Presbyterian. They now gradually became more liturgical, and the Liturgy of 1637, fostered by the Non-jurors, was printed separately after 1724, the edition of

1764 being regarded as the standard. In the 19th century, however, the English Liturgy was generally used in Scotland.

In 1912 a schedule of 'Permissible Additions to and Deviations from the Book of Common Prayer', was issued. In 1918 the revision of the Prayer Book as a whole was begun, and the special committee's proposals were brought at intervals before the Consultative Council. After ten years the work was finished; it was then referred to the Diocesan Synods and to the Consultative Council for acceptance or rejection; and, after almost unanimous acceptance, the new Scottish Prayer Book was duly authorized by the Provincial Synod in 1929. It will be noticed that both in Scotland and in America the methods of revision were thoroughly consultative, and secured general acceptance, thus avoiding the mistakes which so divided the English Church over the Deposited Book as to encourage the House of Commons to reject it.

The Scottish Book gained much from the debates over the English proposals. The Scottish Episcopal Church has for long, like the Eastern Churches, had more than one Liturgy; for both the Scottish and the English Liturgies are included in the Book, and a Canon also allows the Liturgy of the English Deposited Book under certain conditions, 'if and when the Episcopal Synod is satisfied that it has been authorized in the Church of England'.

The Scottish Book adds the Canticle *Benedictus es*, but cuts out of Evensong *Cantate Domino* and *Deus Misereatur*. It contains many new Prayers, prefixed by biddings, versicles, and responses. It contains two Shorter Litanies, one of which is from the old Litany, which is also included, its 'Supplication' being rightly printed as a separate service for times of penitence or trouble. Compline is added, and there are many new Collects, Epistles, and Gospels, as well as Post-Communion and other Collects.

THE CANADIAN PRAYER BOOK

After an abortive attempt which began in 1896 and was continued in 1902, it was decided by the General Synod in 1911 to make a complete revision. Here again the greatest care was taken to consult every one concerned. The result was that in 1921 the Book was finally authorized by a Canon which was passed almost unanimously. The Canadian Prayer Book is a conservative revision embodying certain of those improvements which are now becoming general, and adding new services such as are in the other modern books, with a few others, one for Dominion Day, for instance, and new services for Children and on behalf of Missions. At Morning and Evening Prayer there is a special Prayer for the Governor-General of the Dominion and the Lieutenant-Governors of the Provinces. In addition to the new Prayers and Thanksgiving which we have already mentioned, such as those during Vacancies and during Elections, and the Bidding Prayer, there are Collects, Epistles, and Gospels for the Transfiguration, Rogation Days, and Ember Days. The Canadian Church, like the Protestant Episcopal Church of the United States, suffers under the disadvantage of an official Hymn Book: it was published in 1903 and is 19th century in character.

THE IRISH PRAYER BOOK

The Church of Ireland accepted in 1662 the newly revised English Book. Services were added in the 17th and 18th centuries for the Consecration of Churches, the Visitation of Prisoners, and the Receiving of Converts. From 1800, when the union between England and Ireland was effected, to 1870, the two Churches bore the name of 'The United Church of England and Ireland'. After the disestablishment of 1871, an Irish Prayer Book was published in 1878. In this Book 'according to the Use of the Church of Ireland' the changes were few and unimportant; but Canons were decreed in 1871 and 1877 which deal stringently with ornaments and ceremonial, and are bound up with the Prayer Book.

A revised Prayer Book was begun by the General Synod in 1909. The plates of this new Book were destroyed in the Dublin rising of 1916; but the new Prayer Book at last came into use in 1927. In this Book the Commination and the Visitation of the Sick are recast, and, as in the Scottish and American Books, a separate service for the Burial of a Child is added. The Exhortation, 'Dearly beloved', is allowed to be omitted with the consent of the Ordinary. A new Canticle, *Urbs Fortitudinis* (Isa. 26: 1), is added. There are also Prayers for the Chief Governors in Ireland and for The King and Commonwealth at Morning and Evening Prayer. There is a special Collect, Epistle, and Gospel for the Transfiguration and at the Opening of a Synod. The section of Prayers and Thanksgivings we have mentioned on pp. 141–2.

SOUTH AFRICAN REVISION

Revision in South Africa differs from that in other parts of the Anglican Church in having been carried out by Episcopal Synod since 1911, when it was begun. The Provincial Synod has from time to time ratified what has been done by the Bishops without attempting to revise it. Furthermore, it has not resulted in an entire new Prayer Book. After several revisions an Alternative Communion Service (on the First Model) was finally ratified in 1929. Revision of the Occasional Services was also carried out, as is mentioned in Chapter XVII; and these were published, together with a revised Calendar, in 1930, by the S.P.C.K. The English Lectionary of 1922 is in use.

The Churches of Wales, Australia, and New Zealand have

not at the time of this edition of *The Story of the Prayer Book*, 1933, attempted to revise the Book of 1662 which they use.

48. CONSECRATION OF A CHURCH
St. Mary's, Yenchowfu, Shantung, 1931. The Bishop at the church-door.

In other parts of the Anglican Church the work of revision overlaps with that of translation, and in some parts a good deal of variation naturally results. As we have said, in China and Japan both the English and American books are drawn upon.

On the whole it may be said that the first era of revision is now closing. It has followed certain liturgical fashions, which were the result of the revived study of ancient forms in the 19th century. On the good side the liturgics of the period now closing spread a knowledge of the structure and intention of ancient forms; their defect was an ignoring of theological and philosophical considerations and the tacit assumption that the older anything was the more suitable it must be. People were apt to forget that sometimes the farther back they went, the nearer they were to the Dark Ages; and thus a few tended to become not merely conservative but reactionary. Little was then known about the worship of the Apostolic and the Early Church; and that little was generally ignored, so that it was not realized that some things regarded as very ancient were in fact comparatively late alterations of the original Christian worship. Anglo-Saxon common sense prevented many mistakes from this cause; but it is not unlikely that, great as were the gains from abbreviation and elasticity, the coming generation will complain that some opportunities were missed in the period of the recent revisions. To take two examples of real practical importance: (1) Two of the latest Books still retain 'obey' in the Marriage Service (see p. 241); (2) In some only of the revisions has it been made permissible to omit the concluding section of the *Venite*, and in none to omit that of the *Te Deum*; yet in both cases the canticle is lengthened by an anticlimax, and in neither is the conclusion part of the original form. Other matters more important than these are involved in this era of profound change when our conception of Reality grows and deepens. Many feel increasingly that it may have been a good thing that the attempted revision in England failed, and that the field is still open there for younger men perhaps to combine things new and old in more acceptable proportion, and to meet the needs of a world that will never be the same as that which drew to its end in 1914.

The proposals of the 'Grey Book' towards the close of the work of revision in England showed that a new movement had already begun. Some of these proposals got into the Deposited Book towards the end of the debates, and considerably improved the original draft ('N.A. 84') which in some ways was of second-rate quality and had evoked little enthusiasm. As the years pass, all the revisions so far attempted or carried out in different countries seem to take on an experimental and transitional character, expressing, as they so often do, the ideas of the last century rather than of the present; and it is perhaps more important than we can yet realize that none should rest in what has been done, but that all should be looking forward to a greater work in the future.

PART III

THE SERVICES IN THE PRAYER BOOK

CHAPTER XV
MORNING AND EVENING PRAYER

THIS history would be unfaithful to its modest purpose if it tried to offer the general reader a complete account of the development of our services; since such an account would necessarily be full of those complicated technicalities which make liturgics a forbidding science even to many who are deeply interested in the devotional and artistic aspects of public worship. We must therefore be content with the main outlines, and with these only in so far as they concern the intelligent worshipper of to-day.

First, we must realize the distinct character of the services in which we take part. The old-fashioned type of service obscured this, and people had come to regard the Sunday morning service of Mattins, Litany, Ante-Communion, Sermon, and Hymns as one long and rather shapeless 'liturgy'. They did appreciate its devotional beauty. Let me quote what the saintly Evangelical leader, Charles Simeon, said at the beginning of the 19th century:

'I am never nearer to God than I often am in the reading-desk.' 'As for the Liturgy, no commendation can be too great for it. . . . If a whole assembly were addressing God in the spirit of the Liturgy, as well as in the words, there would be nothing to compare with such a spectacle on the face of the earth; it would approximate more to heaven than anything of the kind that was ever seen in the world.'

If the Evangelical Revival deepened men's sense of this heavenliness of worship, the Tractarian and the Liturgical Movements, which followed in their turn, set forth the beauty and intelligibility of our services. The best and truest parts of these three movements are with us still, purified and strengthened by the work of many who were called Broad Churchmen, and of others, like Maurice, who stood outside the party divisions of the 19th century. The Liturgical Revival helped men to escape from formalism by making the ceremonial itself answer the question, 'What mean ye by this service?' It quickened their spirits by beauty of form, colour, and movement, by making, in fact, the worship of God in the church less unworthy of the work of God in the woods and meadows outside.

We have had, indeed, during recent years, recovery of the art of common and united prayer; and that is why, in spite of some reactions and eccentricities, the so-called High and Low Church parties of the Victorian era are coming together again, each giving up some of its defects, and both merging in the ideal of an evangelical worship carried out with liturgical beauty.

Thus Churchmen as a whole have learned to take a more real and understanding part in our various services, not regarding them as a uniform 'liturgy', performed at the reading-desk, but entering into the spirit of each solemn act of praise or prayer, as each is made clear by its appointed ceremonial. So, to mention the most fundamental point, the different services are held in different places, and have each its own character clearly stamped upon it. The Holy Communion is a great action done solemnly at the altar. Baptism is a service of admission, done at the font near the church door; the Marriage rite is the Christian blessing of the affianced pair, leading them from the body of the church to the Lord's Table; the Commination begins with warning from the pulpit and concludes with penitence when the priest and clerks kneel amidst the people in the nave; the Litany is a special intercession, sung in winding procession through the aisles, to culminate at the chancel-step, or said quietly at a kneeling-desk outside the screen. But Mattins and Evensong are said or sung within the choir, the congregation itself being there accommodated in collegiate churches when there is room. They are thus choir services, and have a different character and object from the rest.

What is this character of *The Divine Service*, as the choir offices are called? It is the daily reading and hearing of Holy

49. CROWCOMBE CHURCH, SOMERSET

An Epitome of Prayer-Book History

The Font is 14th century, the Church 15th century, the aisle 16th century, the pews are dated 1534, the font-cover is 17th century, the screen and the pulpit were made in the time of George I and George II (18th century), and the reredos is Victorian of the 19th century.

Scripture—primarily the recitation of the Psalter, accompanied by prayer and by meditation upon the teaching of the Bible.

This is admirably described in Cranmer's original preface which is still in the English Prayer Book, '*Concerning the Service* [that is the Divine Service] *of the Church*', which states that the English Church set herself to restore 'this godly and decent order of the ancient Fathers', by arranging that the whole Bible should be read through at the daily services, once in the year, and the Psalter continuously recited once a month; for the ancient Fathers had intended

'that the Clergy . . . should (by often reading, and meditation in God's word) be stirred up to godliness themselves, and be more able to exhort others by wholesome doctrine, and to confute them that were adversaries to the truth; and further, that the people (by daily hearing of holy Scripture read in the Church) might continually profit more and more in the knowledge of God, and be the more inflamed with the love of his true religion'.

This ideal was never fully realized; and in the present era the broadcast daily service tends to take the place of the service in parish churches; but it is a noble ideal, and is carried out in our cathedral and collegiate churches and in many others.

The Divine Service is thus now essentially a daily service, just as the Holy Communion is a Sunday and Festival service. And this character takes us far back to the origins of set 'Hours' of worship. We read that Daniel (6: 10) was in the habit of praying three times a day. Much stress was laid in the Middle Ages on certain rather vague passages in the Psalms: 'At midnight I will rise to give thanks unto thee'—'Early in the morning do I cry unto thee'—'Mine eyes prevent the night watches'—and 'Seven times a day do I praise thee'; but, although this was applied to the Seven Canonical Hours of the Christian Church later on, we must remember that the Jews used the number seven merely to suggest frequency or iteration, as in the phrase 'purified seven times in the fire' of the 12th Psalm.

In the Acts of the Apostles we find that the first Christians were like Daniel in observing three hours of prayer. Pentecost, we read in the 2nd chapter, was at the Third Hour; and a picture is given further on of the faithful 'day by day continuing stedfastly with one accord in the Temple, and breaking bread at home', which means probably that they attended the Temple services, and met for friendly meals or agapès in one another's houses. In the 3rd chapter we read of Peter and John 'going up into the Temple at the hour of prayer, being the ninth hour'; and in the 10th chapter, Cornelius and St. Peter see their

visions when praying alone at the 9th and 6th hours respectively. Here, then, are three customary hours of prayer, corresponding with the Terce, Sext, and None, of later ages —the Third Hour of the day (Terce), at 9 a.m.; the Sixth

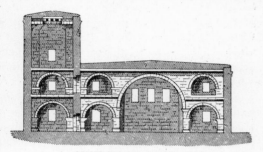

50. CHURCH AT TAFF' KHA

A very early Christian Church at Taff' Kha, in Syria (perhaps of the 3rd century, and the oldest in the world).

Hour (Sext), at noon; and the Ninth Hour (None), at 3 p.m.

We know that these three hours were continued in the early Church; and they are mentioned by Clement of Alexandria and Tertullian (c. A.D. 200) as a recognized custom in Africa. They were at first a matter of private devotion, but gradually a few public services were instituted. The first of these was the Saturday night service, which was kept as a vigil or preparation for the Sunday Eucharist. In this connexion it is worth recalling that many English bishops' charges in the 17th century lay stress on the Saturday Evensong, which is a very good way of preparing for the Lord's Day. In early times this Saturday service was in theory one that lasted all night (as it actually did on Easter Even), and it is still called the All-night Service in Russia and

Greece; but in practice it was generally divided into two—one at lamp-lighting and one at cock-crow—with bedtime in between.

It should be clearly noted that daily services were for long *family prayers*. Daily church services grew up slowly as a result of monasticism. J. H. Maude and Batiffol make this clear, the former (in his *History of the B.C.P.*, 1899) saying that 'The only public services other than the Eucharist, of which there is any evidence during the first three centuries' are 'the vigils of Sundays, the station days, and the birthdays of martyrs'. Bishop J. Wordsworth (in *The Ministry of Grace*, 1901) fixes 'the period 350-75 as that of the introduction of daily public evening and morning prayers into the Eastern Church, followed a few years later by that of Milan'.

At first this was in special centres. The *Pilgrimage of Etheria*, written *c.* A.D. 385, gives an interesting description of the nocturnal service held daily in the Church of the Resurrection at Jerusalem, telling how sets of priests and deacons said prayers between the alternate canticles and psalms with their antiphons, among the monks, virgins, and lay folk, till the bishop came at daybreak; and how other services were held, at the Sixth, Ninth, and Tenth Hours.

To Terce, Sext, and None, by about A.D. 600 (keeping to round numbers for the sake of simplicity), the monks of the West had added two more services—one on rising from bed, called Prime, which was followed by the daily meeting of the Chapter (the business meeting of the monks); the other before going to bed, called Compline, that is the *completion* of the day.

Thus, although in Egypt and other places the monks were still content with the primitive services at lamp-lighting and cock-crow, the monks of the West set themselves to carry out the literal (though not the real) meaning of the Psalmist's words, 'Seven times a day will I praise thee'. But under St. Benedict the Eucharist was still a special service for Sundays and other festivals only. There were in fact eight Hours or Choir Services altogether, which were said at seven different times, the night service of Mattins and the dawn-service of Lauds being said together. They may be set down thus:

NIGHT SERVICE	*Cock-crow*:	3. Nocturns (later called Mattins). ⎞
DAWN SERVICE	*Sunrise*:	4. Lauds (followed directly after ⎟ Nocturns). ⎠
DAY SERVICES	*On rising*:	5. Prime.
	9 *a.m.*:	6. Terce ⎱
	Noon:	7. Sext ⎰ The Little Hours.
	3 *p.m.*	8. None ⎰
EVENING SERVICES	*Sunset*:	1. Vespers (called Evensong in England).
	Bedtime:	2. Compline.

These were the services as they were written down at Rome about the 6th century and adopted in England and many other countries. They consisted almost entirely of portions of the Scriptures: the Psalter was said through each week (not each month only as in our Prayer Book), and there was a regular system of Lessons from the Old and the New Testament. Here was in fact the 'godly and decent order of the ancient Fathers', to which our English Reformers turned for their ideal. With the exception that some Lessons were taken from the Fathers, the only additions to the Bible portions were themselves mainly shorter Scriptural passages: these were the familiar opening Versicles and Responses ('O Lord, open thou', &c.), Responds (appropriate chants sung after the Lessons), Antiphons (appropriate chants, at first after every verse, and later before and after whole Psalms and Canticles); and lastly the *Kyries* and Lord's Prayer with the *Preces* or Suffrages, which formed a little Litany, surviving in our *Kyries*, Lord's Prayer, and the Versicles and Responses, 'O Lord, shew thy mercy upon us', &c.

51. THE OPENING WORDS OF THE PSALTER

'Beatus vir qui non abiit in consilio impiorum.' 'Blessed is the man that hath not walked in the counsel of the ungodly.'

From a Psalter, written at Winchester, probably in the time of Bishop Æthelwald, 963–84.

These eight Hours of the Divine Service in the 8th century were in three groups, as in the following tables. For convenience we add—in small type and square brackets—the main additions of the Medieval Breviary, which will be mentioned next:

I. NOCTURNS (MATTINS)

[Lord's Prayer.]

'O Lord, open thou', &c.

Venite, with Invitatory.

[Metrical Hymn.]

The Nocturn { Psalms, with Antiphons.
℣. and ℟. Lord's Prayer [Creed].
3 Lessons with Responds.

(On Sundays, 3 Nocturns, having in all 18 Psalms and 9 Lessons. On Festivals, 9 Lessons with fewer Psalms.)

[On Festivals, *Te Deum*.]

II. LAUDS, AND VESPERS (EVENSONG)

[Lord's Prayer.]

'O God, make speed', &c.

5 Psalms, with Antiphons.

Short Lesson.

[Metrical Hymn.]

Canticle (at Lauds, *Benedictus*: at Vespers, *Magnificat*), with Antiphon.

Kyries and Lord's Prayer (ferial).

Suffrages (ferial).

[Collect of Day.]

III. THE THREE LITTLE HOURS OF TERCE, SEXT, AND NONE

These were like Lauds and Evensong, but there were only three Psalms (three parts of Ps. 119, for each of the three Little Hours) and no Canticle.

[The Office Hymn was placed before the Psalms, and was invariable.]

PRIME AND COMPLINE

These form a subsidiary group, and may be classed with Groups III and II.

PRIME followed Group III in having three invariable Psalms and no Canticle.

[The Prime Office Hymn followed Group III in position and invariableness.]

COMPLINE was like Group II, but had four invariable Psalms: the Canticle was *Nunc Dimittis*.

[The Compline Office Hymn followed Group II in position and variableness.]

From the 4th century, however, the Divine Service had been becoming purely clerical, and in the West the influence of Rome—strongly practical, but dry and without art or imagination—had grown. Further, by the Middle Ages the service was unintelligible to the people. As a consequence they made up for the loss by 'hearing mass'. New devotions arose; the singing of the Angelus and the use of the rosary were popularized in the 15th century, and the cult of the Saints increased.

Our next point of time is about A.D. 1250, when the revised Hours of the Breviary (p. 37) began to come into use, mainly through the Franciscans. The principal changes in structure were the addition of the Lord's Prayer at the beginning of each service, and of prayers at the end. Metrical hymns—Office Hymns as they are called—had been adopted from the Benedictines. The *Te Deum* had been put into Mattins for festival use; and the Athanasian Creed had been inserted in Prime; memorials and collects of Saints were added at the end of some Hours. Later, the *Ave Maria* (but in its less unscriptural form) came also to be added, though not uniformly. The changes in substance were for the worse and of the most serious character:

the Bible Lessons were reduced, and Lessons from apocryphal stories of the Saints were multiplied.

The decadence continued, as we have explained on pp. 28–36; though indeed we have to remember that in one respect

52. A VILLAGE CHURCH
WHISSENDINE, OAKHAM

53. A VILLAGE CHURCH
LONG SUTTON, LINCS.

this period was beyond praise; to it we owe the matchless churches of Medieval Christendom, churches that were loved and frequented by rich and poor alike, and were furnished by the people with a high sense of beauty. By the time of the Reformation the legendary element was so bad that 'to lie like a second nocturn' became a proverb; and the services— besides being said at inappropriate hours in a language not understood by the people—were in a state of such extraordinary complication that—to repeat our quotation from the preface to the English Prayer Book—'many times there was more business to find out what should be read than to read it when it was found out'.

But this was not all. To the long and intricate Hours yet more was added in the Middle Ages: Commemorations were multiplied; and it became the custom to say or sing in addition a Little Service of the Virgin and the Service of the Dead. To these were sometimes added the Seven Penitential Psalms and the fifteen Gradual Psalms, not to mention the Rosary and other private devotions. Obviously this gradual accretion of poor material had become for many a burden too great to bear. The result was irreverence and neglect. At Exeter, for instance, in 1330, we read of the clerks beguiling the time by pouring wax from their candles on to the shaven heads of those in the lower stalls; and in some cathedrals the canons used to come in at the beginning of service, bow, and walk out again.

The result of all this was the Reformation. So says Cranmer's preface to the Prayer Book, *Concerning the Service of the Church*, which was written before 1549. In place of the Psalter being only recited in part and the Bible read in unintelligent fragments, in place of the 'legends', which really were legends—'some . . . untrue, some uncertain, some vain ,and superstitious'—in place of the confusion caused by the 'number and hardness of the rules called the Pie', the Divine Service was restored to a 'language and order' 'much agreeable to the mind and purpose of the old Fathers'.

How this was done is familiar to every church-goer; and we have' already described, in Chapters V to XIII, the general history of the reform.

We can best show how the old services were combined into our present Mattins and Evensong by the following tables. We

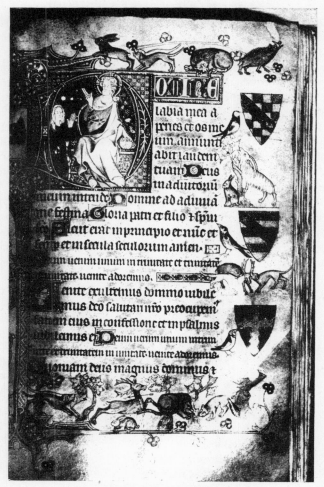

54. 'DOMINE LABIA MEA APERIES'

'O Lord, open thou my lips', &c. The opening Versicles, Responses,
Gloria, *Venite*, &c., of Mattins.

From a particularly fine English MS. Book of Hours, c. 1305.

must, however, bear in mind that such combination was not an innovation in principle: outside the monasteries, the clergy did not attempt to pray seven times a day, but had made two services out of the eight, calling the first six by the general name of Mattins, and the last two (Evensong and Compline) by the general name of Evensong—thus forming a very lengthy and complicated Morning and Evening Prayer.

We have also to remember that the English Service discarded the Office Hymns, Antiphons, and the Responds to the Lessons; and gained by the whole Psalter being said 'in course' for the Psalms, and the whole Bible being read 'in course', in place of the mere snippets which had formed the Lessons of the later Middle Ages. We have now incomparably more fine hymns than the Latin services possessed: few would like to have the Responds back; and though Antiphons may be a beautiful feature, they would probably make the services seem too complicated and obscure for our congregations of lay men and women.

PRAYER BOOK EVENSONG
(Composed in 1549 of the Sarum Evensong and Compline.)

The Sarum Evensong is printed in **Clarendon type.**
The Sarum Compline in Capitals.

Lord's Prayer.
O God, make speed, &c.
Glory be, &c.
Psalms [Antiphons omitted].
Lesson.
[Office Hymn omitted.]
Canticle, Magnificat.
Lesson.
Canticle, Nunc Dimittis.

Added later

Sentences, Exhortn., Confessn., Absoln., 2nd P. B., also 'O Lord, open thou' (from Mattins). (*There had been a Confn. and Absoln. at Compline.*)
(Omission supplied by Hymn Books.)
Alternatives to Canticles, 2nd P. B.

Kyries (Creed added here in 1st P. B.) AND LORD'S PRAYER.

[Confession, &c., omitted.]

SUFFRAGES.

Collect of Day.

Other Collects.

Creed placed before Kyries, *2nd P. B.*

Anthem, and the Five Prayers. 5*th P. B.*, 1661. (*An anthem, e.g. 'Salve Regina', had often been sung after Compline in the pre-Reformation period.*)

PRAYER BOOK MATTINS

(COMPOSED IN 1594 OF THE *SARUM* MATTINS AND LAUDS.)

The Sarum Mattins is printed in **Clarendon type.**

The Sarum Lauds in CAPITALS.

Lord's Prayer.

O Lord, open thou, &c.

O God, make speed, &c.

Glory be, &c.

Canticle, Venite [Invitatory omitted].

[Office Hymn omitted.]

Psalms [Antiphons omitted].

Lesson [Instead of Groups of Lessons with Responds].

Canticle, Te Deum [on Festivals in Sarum use],

or

CANTICLE, BENEDICITE [on Sundays, with Antiphon, in Sarum use].

ADDED LATER

Sentences, Exhortn., Confessn., Absoln., *2nd P. B.* (*There had been a Confn. and Absolution at Prime.*)

(This omission supplied many times over by Hymn Books.)

PRAYER BOOK MATTINS (*continued*)

LESSON.

CANTICLE, BENEDICTUS [Antiphon omitted].

Kyries (from Prime).

Creed (Prime).

Lord's Prayer (Prime).

SUFFRAGES.

COLLECT.

OTHER COLLECTS.

Alternative Canticle, *2nd P. B.*

Creed placed here, *2nd P. B.*

Anthem and the Five Prayers, *5th P.B.*

This, then, is the character of the Divine Service. There are a few prayers in it, or added to it, but in the main it is a service of Psalm and Canticle, of singing and Bible-reading. The Psalter is indeed the very essence of the Service, and has been, as we have seen, ever since the Christian Church sprang from the loins of the Jewish. Mattins and Evensong are Bible Services; for the prayers and metrical hymns are but additions to the solid basis of Holy Scripture, while the sermon and extra hymns added to the Prayer Book service after Sunday Evensong (and in many churches after Mattins also) are merely a popular addition, and form no part of the Prayer Book order.

The Divine Service of the Anglican Church is not incapable of improvement: in the light of modern needs, such as was suggested in the Revision of 1928, all the service, for instance, before 'O Lord, open thou our lips' might be made optional, and we need in these days wider intercessions after the Third Collect; the Lectionary also needs still a thorough revision; but the action of the Reformers has had one remarkable justification. The Divine Service has retained its hold upon the affections of the people, as it has done in no other part of the Catholic Church. Indeed, it is often said that Mattins and

55. A PAGE OF THE EVENSONG OF THE EPIPHANY

From a Franciscan Breviary, the finest 15th-century Florentine work, done in the convent of S. Croce, shortly after the year 1482.

Evensong are too popular, because so many people come to them on Sunday instead of to the Holy Communion. We must not put Mattins into a corner because of this, but must do what we can to make the Holy Communion better understood and loved by eschewing both defect and excess of ceremonial. In the Middle Ages there was hardly any communion, since

56. THE CHOIR OF CARTMEL PRIORY CHURCH
A pre-Reformation screen with returned stalls, remade in the 17th century.

people only communicated once a year; but many kept the Lord's Day holy by attending 'Mattins, Mass, and Evensong'.

It is rather misleading to speak of 'the Lord's own Service', or 'the Lord's Service', as if the phrase excluded Mattins or Evensong; for the worship in which our Lord took part and at which he preached was the Divine Service of the Synagogue, an order of Psalms, Lessons, and Prayers which was the

57. MORNING PRAYER, A.D. 1700

The priest is beginning the service, as the label shows, 'Enter not into Judgement with thy Servant O Lord!' (Morning light). He wears surplice, scarf, and bands; and below him is the clerk wearing bands with a coat of the period. The church is St. Margaret's, Westminster: on the right the Speaker of the House of Commons in his special pew; he is distinguished by his gown, full-bottomed wig, and mace. Other Members of the House of Commons, presumably, are depicted in the gallery. This old print shows the 'three-decker' arrangement, in which the service was taken from the middle desk, the preacher going up to the pulpit for the sermon. The altar is vested on all three sides with a bordered material decorated with an emblem. On it rest the two texts with markers.

pattern upon which the Divine Service of the Christian Church was formed.

Our two Services contribute an invaluable part of the Christian life, a great safeguard against distorted ideas and weak-minded devotions, a great instrument of sobriety, peace, intelligence, and depth in religion. . The Divine Service is a service of quiet and thoughtful worship, of meditation, of learning, remembering, and reflection. There is much rest in it, much time to ponder, and pray, and to relax in God from the strain of mundane life, spreading our souls out in the sunshine of heaven, strengthening our inner life by the fellowship of the Common Prayer, and lifting up tranquil hearts in piety, thankfulness, and resolution to the God of our fathers.

CHAPTER XVI

THE LITANY

WE have the word 'Litany' from the Greek, and 'Rogation' from the Latin, but both words mean the same thing—a service of supplication, though the latter word is now restricted to the processions or other forms of supplication on the three Rogation Days before the Ascension Day.

Litanies existed in the 4th century, or earlier, petitions, that is to say, followed by the Greek words, *Kyrie eleison* ('Lord have mercy')—a pagan form, which was taken over by the Christian Church, at first in the East, in the 4th century; other phrases or responses were added later. Before it came to be used as a separate service, this type of Litany was already in the Byzantine rite a prominent part of the Holy Communion Service: it.still is so, and indeed what strikes the traveller most about the celebration of the Liturgy in Greece or Russia is the deep-voiced deacon, chanting the litanies on the foot-pace in front of the altar-screen, while the choir and people respond. These litanies are comparatively short, as can be seen in two metrical translations, nos. 650 and 652 of the *English Hymnal*. In the West there was anciently a litany sung in procession to the church, a remnant of which is left in the ninefold *Kyrie* ('Lord have mercy, Christ have mercy, Lord have mercy', each repeated thrice at the beginning of the Liturgy), from which come our *Kyries* in the Decalogue ('Lord have mercy upon us, and incline our hearts to keep this law').

There was also a processional service, outside the Liturgy, and associated especially with penitence or particular emergencies. It was in fact what our out-door Rogation processions still are. St. Chrysostom introduced processions with responsorial singing through the streets of Constantinople in 398 as an antidote to the out-door services and processions of the Arians, who had been excluded from the churches and otherwise persecuted by the recent Edicts of Theodosius I. These processions, which were very magnificent, with their silver crosses and wax-

58. PROCESSION TO A TOMB. (A TRANSLATION)

An 11th-century painting at S. Clemente, Rome. Bishop (in albe and chasuble with pallium and mitre), and priests on the left: body of a saint, with four clerks (in albes and tunics) carrying candles in centre: bishop celebrating, with a deacon (in dalmatic), at altar on right.

lights, had some free fights with the Arian processions, and were so popular that they remained as a permanent institution. Thus litanies came to be established for times of plague, famine, earthquake, and other occasions of need. They soon reached the West, and in 477 Mamertus, Archbishop of Vienne in Gaul, ordered litanies to be sung on the three days before Ascension Day, because there had been a disastrous earthquake. From Vienne the custom spread over Gaul. There were also

about the end of this century processions through Rome to
supplant the old annual pagan procession of prayer for the

59. A PROCESSION IN TIME OF WAR, 15TH CENTURY

A bishop preceded by two torch-bearers, and followed by clergy, issuing from
the city gate in the background. A bishop in the foreground approaches the
invading king.

fruits of the earth on April 25th. Thus began the Rogation
Procession, the parent of our English Processional Litany.

This processional type of Litany consisted mainly of Antiphons. As the other type, the stationary dialogue of prayer,
faded out of the Western Liturgies, its features were added to

the processional type; and thus we have the Medieval Litany, a long dialogue of prayer, sung generally in procession.

Meanwhile the emergency use of processions continued. It was natural that in times of need the service of supplication should pass outside the church, and that the clerks should wend their way through the streets which were threatened by war or ravaged by pestilence or famine. On great days other processions would be carried out in much magnificence, the King and Queen, with splendid heralds and officers and mitred bishops, taking their part with the ranks of clergy and people, who proceeded through the winding gabled streets of a medieval city to some old church, grey without and jewelled with colour and lights within; and here a sermon would be preached and Mass said. The ordinary Rogation procession was, however, very simple, and the priest did not, according to the Sarum Processional, wear a cope.

So the Prayer Book Litany was at first often called 'the Procession', whence we find the curious expression after the Battle of Pinkie, 1547, that all the parish churches of London 'kept a solemn procession on their knees in English'.

There was in old England a procession round the church to the high altar, before Mass, on Sundays and Holy-days; there were also processions of this kind at dedications, and after Evensong to the rood, or to the font, or to the altar of a saint; and in Lent a stationary litany was said every day, all kneeling, after Terce.

In 1544 (as we have said on p. 49) Cranmer produced the English Litany, which was the first instalment of the Prayer Book, and which most people consider to be the finest form of prayer in our language. It combines the principal features common to all the old litanies: part is from the Sarum Litany in time of war (England was at war in that year): another part from the Sarum Litany on Rogation Monday, and another part from a German Litany by Luther. The English Litany was first (in 1544) ordered as a special supplication for Wednesdays and Fridays, in view of the French and Scottish wars; in 1545 by royal injunction it superseded the old Procession before

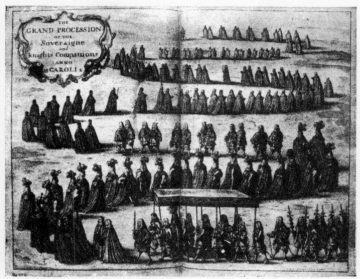

60. PROCESSION OF THE KNIGHTS OF THE GARTER, WITH CLERGY
AND CHORISTERS
From Ashmole's *Institution*, 1672.

Mass; and in 1549 it was ordered to be used always on Wednesdays and Fridays. It was equally suitable for stationary and for processional use, and for special or for ordinary occasions: thus it was ordered to be said 'immediately before the time of communion of the Sacrament', in 1559, when it was also appointed for the 'perambulation of the circuits of parishes' on the Rogation Days. The Rogationtide processional use of the

Litany is frequently mentioned in the bishops' visitation articles of the 17th century, so that the idea of the double use was well established.

We may add a word here about processions in general. They

have naturally been always used for utilitarian purposes, as, for instance, when a body was carried to the tomb, or when candidates were brought to the font. They also have a place as special acts of prayer and praise. Until 1549 processions of the latter sort were sung before the Eucharist on festivals, especially the different versions of *Salve festa dies* ('Hail thee, festival day', the examples in the *English Hymnal* being nos. 624, 628, 630, 634, which are condensed in *Songs of Praise*, no. 389); the First Prayer Book has a rubric allowing for some such substitution, and indeed Cranmer had made some experimental translations. Thus in the Prayer Book the only processions specifically ordered besides the Litany are that to the font for Baptism after the Second Lesson (for which no words are provided), that to the Holy Table at Weddings (for which two psalms are provided), and the two connected with the Burial of the Dead, for the first of which Sentences are given. In the 19th century the Hymn Books supplied the want, and processions (largely regarded at first as a cheerful way of entering church, and devoid of stations for prayer) became very popular on festivals. Other processions, however, were in use before the modern popular revival, as those for Rogationtide, mentioned above, for instance, or that shown on p. 175; and at the coronation of a sovereign there was always a procession of special magnificence in Westminster Abbey. In the present century the use of the Litany in procession on ordinary Sundays or on special days

62. A PROCESSION IN AFRICA TO-DAY
At the dedication of St. Peter's, Rosettenville, Transvaal.

has been revived. Churchmen, however, were still very shy about proceeding out of doors, and did very little in this direction till the Salvation Army and the Church Army had familiarized the whole Empire with the idea.

We can explain the origin and structure of the Litany in tabular form, first reminding the reader that the Medieval Litanies (as far back as Anglo-Saxon times) contained many invocations of the Saints after the opening invocation of the Holy Trinity, each having the refrain 'Ora pro nobis'. Cranmer, in 1544, reduced these invocations to three—(1) Saint Mary, (2) the Angels, and (3) 'All holy patriarchs, and prophets, apostles, martyrs, confessors, and virgins, and all the blessed

N

company of heaven, *Pray for us*'. These were omitted in 1549 from the First Prayer Book.

I. THE INVOCATIONS

'*O God the Father*', . . . concluding with the petition *Remember not, Lord . . .*

Spare us, good Lord.

SOURCES

Litanies in general. Sarum Antiphon to Penitential Psalms.

II. THE SUFFRAGES

1. The Deprecations
(against evil).

From all evil . . . to *. . . Word and Commandment.*

Good Lord, deliver us.

2. The 'Obsecrations'
(entreaties that we may be delivered by the power of Christ).

By the mystery . . . to *. . . day of judgement.*

Good Lord, deliver us.

Various ancient sources: Sarum Processional (Litany for Rogation Monday), —with some parts (especially the Intercessions after *unity, peace, and concord*) from a Litany by Luther of 1529.

3. The Intercessions
(for others).

We sinners do beseech . . . to *. . . turn their hearts.*

We beseech thee to hear us, good Lord.

As above, mainly from Luther's Litany.

4. The Two Supplications
(for ourselves).

That it may please . . . kindly fruits of the earth . . . to *according to thy holy Word.*

We beseech thee to hear us, good Lord.

1. Sarum and Luther.
2. Original.

III. THE KYRIE AND THE LORD'S PRAYER

Invocations.

Son of God . . . to O Christ, hear us.

Kyrie.

Lord, have mercy upon us . . .

Lord's Prayer.

Our Father . . .

Concluding ℣. ℟. and Collect.

Priest. *O Lord, deal not . . .*

Let us pray. O God, merciful Father . . .

IV. THE SECOND LITANY

('THE SUPPLICATION')

Processional Anthem with Psalm verse.

O Lord, arise . . . to
As it was in the beginning . . .

Versicles.

From our enemies . . . to graciously hear us, O Lord Christ.

Concluding ℣. ℟. and Prayers.

Priest. *O Lord, let thy mercy . . .*

Let us pray. We humbly beseech . . .

Prayer of St. Chrysostom.

The Grace.

The Prayer of St. Chrysostom is taken from the Eastern Liturgy of St. Chrysostom, where it is said (as in that of St. Basil) by the priest during the Deacon's Litany in the first part of the Liturgy. It was translated by Cranmer for the English Litany, being thus by him intended to be used in its original eucharistic connexion; and it therefore belongs properly to the Litany, and not to the Divine Service. It was not till the last Revision in 1662 that it was placed at the end of Mattins and Evensong, a proceeding which might suggest a certain poverty of invention if the prayer were not such a beautiful one.

Thus the Prayer Book Litany, while it combines the two original objects of processions—prayer against evils and dangers and prayer for the fruits of the earth—greatly extends the realm of intercession, stretching out those touching and melodious phrases, which are now of the very marrow of the English language, to all human needs, dangers, sorrows, aspirations, and efforts towards perfection, and ending with the two beautiful supplications in which the people turn at length to pray for their own necessities. In contrast to the tedious iteration of the Latin Litanies and to the weak and selfish spirit of many popular modern devotions, we think proudly of the English Litany, and have a right to be proud of it. We are indeed brought to the centre of our worship through a noble gate, through the preparation of that generous, unselfish, and humble intercession for the human race which the Litany has given us; and it is our own fault if our religion falls behind the fullness of the Gospel of Christ.

CHAPTER XVII
THE HOLY COMMUNION

RECENT discoveries and studies have shown that the origins of the Holy Communion service are less simple than had been generally supposed. The question of the Institution is a very difficult one, upon which scholars are not yet agreed: and the resemblance between the Lord's Supper of the early Church and the Liturgy of the Middle Ages is so slight that we have to remove from our minds most of the ideas connected even with the Reformed services before we can understand the Eucharist or Agapè in the age of the Apostles. Simple statements are apt to be misleading; but we can say one quite simple thing with certainty—that the first Christians met for a friendly meal; and that this meal, certainly in St. Paul's experience, included a grace or thanksgiving which was a fellowship or participation in the body and blood of Christ.

THE LAST SUPPER AND THE LORD'S SUPPER

To study the matter needs a good deal of reading in Greek, German, and other languages, for in England we have been behindhand with literature on the subject (though much may be gleaned from such a book as Dr. Oesterley's *Jewish Background of the Christian Liturgy*); but it will help us to understand if we remember one very simple fact—that words used of New Testament worship must be taken in their plain meaning and not in any later more developed ecclesiastical sense. For instance, 'eucharist' means thanksgiving (as indeed it is translated in our Bibles), 'communion' means fellowship or participation; and the 'Lord's Supper' means what it says, an evening meal in the name of the Lord—not what we now understand by a 'service'. This 'love-feast' came to be called an Agapè, and towards the middle of the 2nd century the Agapè came to be separated from the Eucharist—that is from the special thanksgiving over bread and wine. In the Apostolic age the Lovefeast and the Thanksgiving (the Eucharist) are one and the same thing: when we read of the Lord's Supper we can for clearness use the term Agapè-Eucharist. The 'breaking of bread' in Acts may mean the same thing; but some authorities think the phrase is to be taken literally, as not including the cup: and there is not yet agreement on the subject.

The question whether our Lord actually instructed the disciples to observe this common meal in his memory is not an easy one. The four accounts in the first three Gospels and I Corinthians 11 differ widely: they have indeed only six words in common. St. Paul seems to say that his account was not obtained from an eyewitness (1 Cor. 11: 23). The four texts must be studied in parallel columns and compared. Many think that St. Mark's account is nearest to the original tradition. Westcott and Hort treat 'This do in remembrance of me', in the present conflated text of St. Luke, with the mention of the cup in 5: 20, as a later addition. St. Mark does not give these words; but St. Paul's account is the earliest, and he considered that they had been said in order that the Agapè-Eucharist should be a memorial of the Lord's death. Thus he says in 1 Cor. 11: 23, as translated in Moffat's version, 'This cup means the new covenant ratified by my blood; as often as you drink it, do it in memory of me'.

The representation of our Lord as a law-giver who laid down rules and established set services no longer holds the assent of scholars. But one other fact is certain, and it is enough: the Jews had a custom of taking a simple meal together solemnly and with prayer; the Last Supper was literally the *last* of these suppers in the Apostolic circle at which Jesus presided and blessed God and gave thanks. Whether an explicit command was given or not, it was inevitable that the Disciples should continue to break bread solemnly together after our Lord's Ascension.

The reader can study the New Testament references to the Agapè-Eucharist for himself, with the use of recent commentaries such as every one ought to possess. There are five passages in which the breaking of bread is mentioned:

And they continued steadfastly in the apostles' teaching and fellowship, in the breaking of bread and the prayers. (Acts 2: 42.)

And day by day, continuing steadfastly with one accord in the temple, and breaking bread at home, they did take their food with gladness and singleness of heart, praising God. (Acts 2: 46.)

And upon the first day of the week, when we were gathered together to break bread, Paul discoursed with them, intending to depart on the morrow; and prolonged his speech until midnight. (Acts 20: 7.)

We have already referred to the fourth passage, 1 Cor. 10: 15–17, 'The cup of blessing which we bless, is it not a communion of the blood of Christ? The bread which we break, is it not a communion of the body of Christ?' The fifth follows in the next chapter (1 Cor. 11: 20–34), where St. Paul rebukes the Corinthians for excesses at the Agapè and goes on to speak of the sacred nature of the meal, which he illustrates, as we have said, by his account of the Last Supper. In the next earliest documents we possess we find the same indication of the Agape culminating in the thanksgiving or Eucharist.

Much early evidence must have been destroyed in the Dark Ages and after, when much also was fabricated. But in 1875 a surviving copy was discovered of the *Didachè* ('The Teaching of the Twelve Apostles'): at first many were puzzled, because

little was then known about the Agapè, and some thought that
the book must have come from an out-of-the-way corner of the
Church. But it is, on the contrary, central and of a date probably before the year 100; and it was so highly esteemed in the
Early Church that it was not far from inclusion in the canon
of the New Testament. In the *Didachè* we find, as in St. Paul's
epistle, the Agapè-Eucharist; and in it is also the earliest
liturgical prayer. The chapters are not connected, and for convenience we will quote cap. xiv first:

'On the Lord's Day of the Lord, when ye are assembled,
break bread and give thanks' (*eucharistesate*).

Here 'break bread' must mean 'eat your meal', i.e. the Agapè.
Next chapter x refers to the Agapè and proceeds to give a
prayer for the thanksgiving (or Eucharist) with which it concludes:

'After ye are filled, thus give thanks (*eucharistesate*): "We
give thanks to thee, Holy Father, for thy holy name which
thou didst make to tabernacle in our hearts, and for the
knowledge and faith and immortality which thou didst make
known to us, through Jesus Christ thy servant. To thee be
glory for ever. Thou, Lord all-ruling, didst create all things
for thy name's sake, and didst give food and drink to men
for their enjoyment that they might give thanks to thee; but
us thou hast blest with spiritual food and drink and eternal
light through thy servant." '

This thanksgiving concludes with a petition for deliverance
from evil, and 'Hosanna', and 'If any be holy, let him come;
if not, let him repent. Maran atha. Amen.' And chapter ix
gives another eucharistic passage:

'And concerning the thanksgiving (*eucharistias*) thus give
thanks (*eucharistesate*). First concerning the cup: "We give
thanks to thee, our Father, for the holy vine of David thy
servant, which thou didst make known to us through thy

servant Jesus. To thee be glory for ever." And concerning
that which was broken: "We give thanks to thee, our Father,
for the life and knowledge which thou didst make known to
us through thy servant Jesus. To thee be glory for ever."
"As this broken bread was scattered upon the mountains,
but was brought together and became one, so let thy Church
be gathered together from the ends of the earth into thy
Kingdom; for thine is the glory and the power through Jesus
Christ for ever." '

The cup, it will be noticed, comes first in this passage, as it
does in St. Paul's account. There is no reference at all to the
Last Supper.

The next mention of the Agapè-Eucharist is in St. Ignatius's
Epistle to the Smyrnaeans (viii), about A.D. 115, where the two
things are mentioned in such a way that they might very well
be one and the same. Ignatius says, 'Let that be accounted a
valid Eucharist which is under the bishop or one whom he
appoints'; and in the next passage he says, 'It is not lawful
either to baptize or to hold an Agapè without a bishop'.

About the same time, in 112, Pliny sent the following account
to the Emperor Trajan of the Christians in the remote province
of Bithynia, where he was governor. Pliny as a pagan writes
vaguely; but certain points emerge. These Christians met early
for the primitive 'cock-crow' hymn. Pliny also notes that, so
far from being criminals, they swore (at a time not specified) to
abstain from crime, by a solemn oath. (The Latin for oath is
sacramentum; and Pliny naturally uses this word: it would not
have been used by the Bithynians themselves, for they were
Greek-speaking; nor was the Latin word applied to any Christian ordinances till three or four generations later.) They then
dispersed; and later in the day assembled again for a meal which
may have been the Agapè-Eucharist:

'They maintained that all their fault or error was this, that they had been accustomed on a fixed day to meet before dawn and sing antiphonally a hymn to Christ as to a god; and that they bound themselves by a solemn oath, not for any crime, but to abstain from theft, brigandage, and adultery, to keep their word, and not to refuse to restore a deposit when demanded. After this was done, they dispersed and assembled again to share a common meal of innocent food; and even this, they said, they had given up after I had issued the edict by which, in accordance with your instructions, I prohibited the existence of clubs.'

RECENTLY DISCOVERED PICTURES

Some years ago—in 1894—Monsignor Wilpert made the intensely interesting discovery of a picture of the Eucharist (or Agapè-Eucharist) of about the same time as Pliny's rescript, that is, between A.D. 100 and 150—the first quarter of the second century is Wilpert's estimate. The picture (reproduced here as Fig. 63), which he calls *Fractio Panis*, the Breaking of Bread, is on the walls of a chapel in the Roman catacomb of Priscilla. It represents the president, wearing over his tunic the teacher's *pallium* (which had much the same significance as the M.A. gown of to-day), seated at one end of a table in the act of breaking, with some show of force, a small roll. Round the table there sit or recline five other men (in tunic without the *pallium*) and one woman. The presence of a woman, together with the general character of this and the later pictures, shows that no representation of the Last Supper is intended. The table is covered with a white cloth; and on it can be discerned a two-handled mug-shaped cup and a plate with five more of the small loaves or rolls. Also on the table, in the middle and in front, is another plate with two fishes.

Are these fishes merely symbolic? The fish was of course an early symbol of Christ; and it was connected in these early

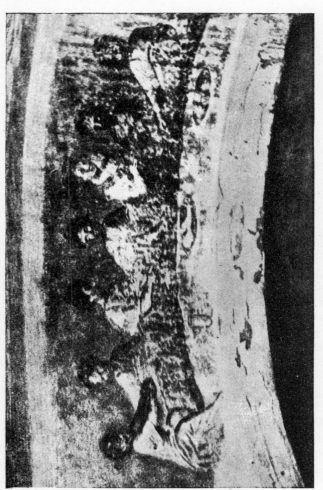

63. THE EUCHARIST AT THE BEGINNING OF THE SECOND CENTURY

From the Catacomb of Priscilla, Rome, called by Wilpert 'Fractio Panis', the earliest of the 'rappresentazioni eucaristiche'

Six people sit quietly while the president on the left, wearing a pallium, breaks the bread for the eucharistic Thanksgiving, probably at the end of an Agapè. On the table is a dish with two fishes, and right and left of this are a plate of rolls and a cup. The fourth figure from the president is that of a woman. Outside our reproduction, on either side of the group, is a symbolical row of seven baskets containing rolls of bread.

catacomb frescoes with the Feeding of the Five Thousand, the Eucharist, and Baptism. On the other hand, it is difficult to suppose that a plate of fried fish was such a symbol; and the mere presence of such an object in this and the later frescoes shows that people were used to seeing on the Lord's table other food besides bread and wine. Moreover, in a small picture, easily missed (Wilpert, 272), not later than the second half of the 2nd century, one figure is cutting up a fish, while others are holding out their hands for helpings. In that case the plate of fishes is certainly part of the meal; and the correct conclusion seems to be that this is so in all the instances; and that *Fractio Panis* therefore represents the Agapè as well as the Eucharist.

Beyond the group, and outside the main picture on either side, are seven baskets filled with rolls of bread, with an obvious reference to the Feeding of the Multitude. Here, then, is a contemporary picture of the sacred meal of the Early Church, as it was actually celebrated at a funeral in this underground chapel (the normal celebrations of the Lord's Supper were held above ground in private houses): a stone bench is still there to-day, and a small tomb, the size of which suggests the scanty remains of some martyr; but the stone over the tomb, which may have served as a table, is gone.

This is reproduced in colour as Plate 15 of Wilpert's *Roma Sotterannea*; on the same page is a similar picture, of the end of the 2nd century, which we have reproduced as Fig. 64 on p. 189, with seven people reclining round the cushions of the *sigma*, one fish on the table (the plate with bread being mutilated in this fresco, where the hole may obliterate a cup also), and ten baskets of bread on either side.

There are reproduced in Wilpert's huge book two other similar 2nd-century *Rappresentazioni eucaristiche* on Plate 41; and on one of these the fishes and the loaves are on the same dish. No cup is shown on these two frescoes. The frescoes

64. THE AGAPÈ AT THE END OF THE SECOND CENTURY

From the Catacomb of Callistus, Rome

The gestures of some of the figures suggest the Agapè rather than the eucharistic Thanksgiving. Owing to the mutilated condition of the wall we cannot know whether there was a cup and bread originally or not. There is a fish on a dish at one side, and on the other a similar dish on which the ends of a second fish can be discerned. There are seven persons, grouped round the sigma or cushion, the middle figure being apparently that of the president. On either side of the group are ten baskets of bread.

of the 3rd and 4th century, on the other hand, may suggest, as we should expect, that the Agapè had by then become a separate meal; they are reproduced by Wilpert as Plates 65, 133, 157, 184, and 267, though the last (of the second half of the 4th century) is still called by him *Banchetto eucaristico*, while the title *Banchetto celeste* is suggested for Nos. 157 and 184. In fact, after the 2nd century, the identification becomes uncertain; and Plate 62 shows a lady and her maid in the 3rd century buying vegetables at a greengrocer's for what is evidently a funeral Agapè pure and simple.

CONTINUANCE OF THE AGAPÈ-EUCHARIST

We have to remember carefully that the Churches varied greatly during the first six or seven centuries. The separation of the Eucharist from the Agapè may, as we shall see, have begun in Rome; but elsewhere it came later. It is sometimes said that Tertullian's account in his *Apology* (cap. 39) shows that the separation had occurred in Africa by his time, *c.* 200; but the *Encyclopaedia Britannica* is justified in saying in its last edition that his account 'is not, perhaps, exclusive of an accompanying eucharist'; though he does not use words like 'sacrament' in their later technical sense, but calls the Eucharist *coetus et congregatio*, and uses the words *coena* and *coenula* for the Agapè. He speaks of the Agapès as 'entertainments' (*refrigerio*), and immediately proceeds: 'We do not lie down at table until prayer has been offered to God, as it were a first taste. We eat only to appease our hunger . . . After washing our hands and lighting the lamps, each is invited to sing before all a hymn to God, either taken from Holy Writ or of his own composition. So we prove him, and see how well he has drunk. Prayer ends, as it began, the banquet.' This may quite well mean that in Africa the Eucharist had come to precede, instead of following, the evening Agapè, as a 'first taste'; and the order would then be, 1. Eucharist, 2. Agapè, 3. Concluding hymns and prayers.

In any case Tertullian describes the Agapè as a religious meal at which every one ate and drank temperately according to their needs, and the poor were entertained as well; the conversation, he says, was discreet and pious; the whole proceeding was a means of drawing people more closely together. But when Tertullian became a Montanist, his violent nature rebounded, and he described the Agapès of the orthodox Christians in flagrant terms. From other books we learn that his wife followed a superstitious practice of the time in keeping a portion of the consecrated bread at home in a box, and nibbling a little before every meal (which was done as a prophylactic against poison); and also that in time of persecution the Eucharist was celebrated in the middle of the night instead of in the evening.

About the same time, and in Egypt, St. Clement of Alexandria (who died in 210) condemns 'little suppers which were called, not without presumption, *Agapè*', and says that the word should be used, not for mere junketings, but for the Eucharist. This seems to point in the same direction.

The most striking fact is that in the 5th century the Agapè-Eucharist still survived in some districts round Alexandria and in the conservative Thebaid. In his *History of the Church* (5 : 22) Socrates, who died *c.* 445, records the fact, which to him seemed singular, that in these places the love-feast was combined with the Eucharist.

Meanwhile, in the Byzantine Church, we find still some connexion, in a passage of St. Chrysostom (*Hom.* 54)—he died in 407—where he describes how, when the Eucharist was over, a banquet was held in church, the rich bringing meat and drink and entertaining the poor. In some churches, however, Agapès in church were already forbidden, as by the Council of Laodicea, A.D. 363, and at Carthage, under the influence of Augustine;

but nothing of a more general nature was done till the prohibition by the Council in Trullo, A.D. 692.

Thus the Agapè still existed at the end of the 7th century. We hear of it still in the 8th in Armenia; and here, strangely enough, as in the Persian and Georgian Churches, it was connected with animal sacrifices. Nay, this was also the case in Italy and Gaul; and Paulinus of Nola describes such sacrifices as Agapès in his poems, *c.* 400. Stranger still, St. Gregory the Great sent to St. Mellitus, Bishop of London, a written rite for the sacrificing of bulls for use in the English Church, in the 7th century.

THE SEPARATE DEVELOPMENT OF THE EUCHARIST

Thus the separation of the Agapè and its eventual disappearance came later in some Churches than in others. It may well be that in Rome by the middle of the 2nd century the Eucharist was distinct from it. At least there is no hint of an Agapè in Justin Martyr's *Apology* to the Emperor Antoninus Pius, A.D. 155; and although we must admit the possibility that Justin did not think it wise to confuse the Emperor's mind by describing more than was necessary, the mere fact that the Agapè is not mentioned at all shows that it could not have held the important position that had belonged to it fifty years before. The Eucharist described by Justin was held on a Sunday, and late enough in the day for people to have come in from the surrounding country. We may conjecture with some probability that the visitors were entertained and that there was therefore some kind of friendly meal or meals; but that is all.

Moreover, the Christian population of Rome was by then so large that it is difficult to conceive how so intimate a gathering as the primitive Agapè-Eucharist could have been managed by the general congregations; not many people could be accommodated in the old way of reclining in a semicircle with

a tripod in the midst. The method must somehow have been
extended, except in the case of small bodies of devout people;
and as the century went on, the crowds that gathered in a large
city round the Lord's table must have sooner or later caused
the meal to develop into what we now call a service. Certainly
the action that Justin describes had a marked liturgical character, even when we take care not to read into it later liturgical
ideas.

Here, then, is Justin's account, which for clearness I venture
to provide with headings, to show that subsequent developments were extensions of the same main divisions:

JUSTIN MARTYR, A.D. 155
Part I
1. *The Preparation*

LESSONS.

'On the day called Sunday, all those who live in the towns
or in the country meet together; and the memoirs of the
Apostles or the writings of the Prophets are read, as long as
time allows.

SERMON.

'Then, when the reader has ended, the president addresses
words of instruction and exhortation to imitate these good things.

Part II
2. *The Offertory*

PRAYER.

'Then we all stand up together and offer prayers.' [In another
place: 'In common for ourselves and for the illuminated [i.e.
baptized, persons] and for all others in every place, that we may
be counted worthy, now that we have learned the truth, by

o

our work also to be found good citizens and keepers of the commandments, so that we may be saved with an everlasting salvation.']

KISS OF PEACE (here or later).

[In another part of his *Apology*, Justin speaks of the Kiss as between the Prayers and the Offertory: 'We salute one another with a kiss, when we have concluded the prayers.']

BRINGING OF THE ELEMENTS.

'And when prayer is ended, bread is brought and wine and water.'

[In another place he writes of this: 'Bread and a cup of wine mingled with water are then brought to the president of the brethren.']

3. *The Thanksgiving*

(The Eucharistic Prayer)

'And the president offers up prayers and thanksgivings alike with all his might.'

[It will be remembered that no details are given by Justin. The word 'thanksgivings' above is *eucharistias* in the original Greek, as in the *Didachè*. Thus the word for thanksgiving came in after years to be given to the whole service.]

'And the people give their assent, saying the *Amen*.

4. *The Communion*

'And the distribution of the elements, over which thanksgiving has been uttered, is made, so that each partakes.' [In another place he says: 'And when the president has given thanks and all the people have expressed their assent, those who are called by us "deacons" give each of those present the bread, and wine mixed with water, over which the thanksgiving was pronounced, and they carry away a portion to those who were not present.']

Justin Martyr's description concludes as follows:

'And to those who are absent they are sent by the hands of deacons. And those who have the means, and are so disposed, give as much as they will, each according to his inclination; and the sum collected is placed in the hands of the president, who himself succours the orphans and widows, and those who through sickness or any cause, are in want, and the prisoners, and the foreigners who are staying in the place; and, in short, he provides for all who are in need.'

THE BASILICAN COMPROMISE

We have noted the large numbers gathering round the Lord's table as the Christian population increased. It is not difficult to imagine how this led to the basilican arrangement which must have been usual in the 3rd century and was the established system in the 4th. Imagine a congregation assembled in the dining-room or the *atrium* of a private house. The people are now too numerous to do anything but stand: at the farther side of the table is the president and some presbyters, for whom, being few in number, sitting accommodation in a semicircle can be found: on the near side some deacons stand and move about, assisting at the service and distributing the elements after the thanksgiving; and nearer to the door stand the congregation. Here is the germ of the basilican service. We can get an idea of it on a small scale in the reconstruction of the original chapel in the catacomb of Callistus, Fig. 65, though screens are unlikely in the earlier ages of transition.

Then a special church is built: in the apse is a central seat for the president or bishop; round him sit the presbyters: on the chord of the apse is the Lord's table; round this move the deacons assisting at the service; and in what is now the nave the people are standing.

The bishop now came forward to the table for the solemn

prayers, and stood facing the people; but, later on, in the fully developed basilican plan, he was hidden by curtains drawn round the *ciborium* or canopy over the altar. This arrangement (without the curtains), a silent witness to a long forgotten past, is still to be seen in the basilicas of Rome. At Canterbury also the archbishop's throne was still behind the altar until it was ignorantly moved in the nineteenth century; and at Norwich a bishop's seat has recently been discovered in the east wall of the cathedral, and is now visible in its commanding position behind the altar. Just these few traces remain of the earlier stages of transition.

65. CHAPEL IN THE CATACOMB OF CALLISTUS
Restored as it probably was in the 4th century.

Knowledge about the subject has not yet been very generally

assimilated. When it is, there should be a happy reduction of controversy; for some issues will have lost their vitality, and some arguments will begin to seem a little insincere. Many phrases and contentions, once used and discussed on one side or the other, have become irrelevant; and, as our knowledge of the New Testament grows profounder and more exact, we are able to draw together with more confidence as the mind of the Christ of the Upper Room is increasingly revealed.

What is past can never indeed be reconstructed: for all the conditions are changed. We should not meet with any success if we attempted to revive the love-feast in the form with which St. Paul was familiar; but we might find new means of drawing the people of our parishes more closely together; and we might indeed increase the religious character of all our meals. And we may expect that any future revisions of our Liturgies may take a further direction in the light of the new knowledge, and may place a fresh emphasis on the thought of fellowship in the One Bread, which is so prominent both in the *Didachè* and in St. Paul.

LITURGICAL DEVELOPMENT

There are some relics in Justin Martyr's account of what we find in the writings of St. Paul. The Kiss of Peace is mentioned in Romans 16: 16; 1 Corinthians 16: 20; 2 Corinthians 13: 12 (and also in 1 Peter 5: 14). There was also reading, for St. Paul's own letters were read to the Churches. The Old Testament was familiar; and in Acts 20: 7 a sermon is mentioned because St. Paul preached on that occasion for so long that his discourse lasted till after midnight. Also we learn from 1 Corinthians 14: 16 that the custom of saying *Amen* was established in connexion with thanksgiving.

The prayers were extemporary, though they came to follow accustomed lines. As time went on some found it more convenient to write down the prayers they used; and it was in this way that fixed rituals grew up. We know that one bishop did this *c.* 350; for there was discovered in the Greek monastery of Mount Athos, and published in 1899, a collection of prayers by an Egyptian bishop, Sarapion, who was a friend of St. Athanasius. In this book, which has been translated by the late Bishop of Salisbury, Dr. Wordsworth (*Bishop Serapion's Prayer Book,* 1899), we have the earliest known Eucharistic Prayer or Anaphora, and a very beautiful one it is. The Church of to-day, Greek, Russian, Latin, or English, has lost as well as gained since Sarapion wrote down his prayers in the Delta of the Nile.

It will be noticed that there is a reference to the gathering together of the bread once scattered upon the mountains, as in the *Didachè.* In the *Didachè* there is no reference to the Last Supper; but here, if it is not regarded as a formal institution, it is at least looked to as an example, though the words 'Do this in remembrance of me' do not occur.

THE ANAPHORA OF SARAPION

The Preface

It is meet and right to praise, to hymn, to glorify thee the uncreated Father of the only-begotten Jesus Christ. We praise thee, O uncreated God, who art unsearchable, ineffable, incomprehensible to every created substance. We praise thee who art known of thy Son the only begotten, who through him wast uttered and interpreted and made known to created nature. We praise thee who knowest the Son and revealest to the saints the glories that are about him: who art known of thy begotten Word, and art brought to the sight and interpreted to the understanding of the saints. We praise thee, O invisible Father, provider of immortality. Thou art the fount of life, the fount of light, the fount of all grace and all truth, O Lover of men, O Lover of the poor, who reconcilest thyself to all, and drawest all to thyself through the sojourning of thy beloved Son. We beseech thee, make us living men. Give us a spirit of light, that we may know thee the true, and him

whom thou didst send, even Jesus Christ. Give us the Holy Spirit
that we may be able to tell forth and to relate thine unspeakable mys-
teries. May the Lord Jesus speak in us and the Holy Spirit, and hymn
thee through us.

For thou art far above all principality and power and might and
dominion, and every name that is named, not only in this world but
also in that which is to come. Before thee stand thousand thousands,
and myriad myriads of angels, archangels, thrones, dominations,
principalities, powers; before thee stand the two most honourable six-
winged seraphim, with two wings covering the face, and with twain
the feet, and with twain flying, and crying, 'Holy', with whom receive
also our cry of 'holy' as we say:

The Sanctus

Holy, holy, holy, Lord of Sabaoth, full is the heaven and the earth
of thy glory.

The Eucharistic Prayer

[*Oblation.*] Full is the heaven, full is also the earth of thy excellent
glory, Lord of Hosts. Fill also this sacrifice with thy power and thy
participation: for to thee have we offered this living sacrifice, the un-
bloody oblation. To thee we have offered this bread the likeness of the
body of the Only-begotten.

[*Narrative of the Last Supper.*] This bread is the likeness of the holy
body, for the Lord Jesus Christ in the night in which he was betrayed
took bread and brake and gave to his disciples, saying, 'Take and eat,
this is my body which is being broken for you for the remission of sins'.
Wherefore we also making the likeness of the death have offered the
bread, and we beseech thee through this sacrifice be reconciled to all
of us and be merciful, O God of truth: and as this bread had been
scattered on the top of the mountains, and, gathered together, came
to be one, so also gather thy holy Church out of every nation and every
country and every city and village and house, and make one living
catholic Church, We have offered also the cup, the likeness of the
blood, for the Lord Jesus Christ, taking a cup after supper, said to his
own disciples, 'Take, drink, this is the new covenant, which is my
blood, which is being shed for you for remission of sins.' Wherefore
we have also offered the cup, presenting a likeness of the blood.

[*The Epiklesis or Consecration.*] O God of truth, let thy holy Word
come to sojourn on this bread that the bread may become body of the

Word, and on this cup that the cup may become blood of the Truth.
And make all who communicate to receive a medicine of life for the
healing of every sickness and for the enabling of all advancement and
virtue, not for condemnation, O God of truth, and not for censure and
reproach. For we have invoked thee, the uncreated, through the Only-
begotten in the Holy Spirit.

[*The Intercession.*] Let this people receive mercy, let it be counted
worthy of advancement, let angels be sent forth as companions to the
people for bringing to nought of the evil one and for establishment
of the Church.

We intercede also on behalf of all who have fallen asleep, whose is
also the memorial we are making. (*After the recitation of the names*):
Sanctify these souls; for thou knowest all. Sanctify all souls at rest in
the Lord. And number them with all thy holy hosts and give them a
place and a mansion in thy kingdom.

Receive also the thanksgiving of the people, and bless those who
offered the oblations and the thanksgivings, and grant health and
soundness and cheerfulness and all advancement of soul and body to
this whole people through the only-begotten Jesus Christ in the Holy
Spirit; as it was, and is, and shall be to generations of generations
and to all the ages of the ages. *Amen.*

Here we find an Epiklesis or Invocation, though it is an
invocation of 'thy holy Word'. First, the bread and cup are
offered as a likeness of the body and blood because there is
being made a likeness of the death; then follows the Epiklesis,
couched in mystical terms, the celebrant praying that the holy
Word may sojourn on the bread and the cup, that they may be
'body of the Word' and 'cup of the Truth'.

It was indeed in the 4th century that the Epiklesis developed
into a definite prayer that the Holy Spirit would descend upon
the elements. Originally the Eucharistic Prayer was a thanksgiving: as time went on, the so-called Words of Institution
and the Epiklesis were added; though some liturgies continued
to be without the former, and some without the latter.

Extracts from early documents illustrating the development
can be found in Professor Oesterley's *Jewish Background of*

the Christian Liturgy (1925). In the 1st and 2nd centuries (*Didachè*, Justin Martyr Irenaeus) there is no Epiklesis. In the 3rd century (Tertullian, Origen, Cyprian, and others) there are prayers for the descent of the Spirit upon the worshippers, but not upon the elements. In the 4th century (*Apostolic Constitutions*, *Canons of Hippolytus*, *Testament of our Lord*) the Epiklesis begins to appear, but it is indefinite, as in Sarapion whom we have quoted—with the exception of Cyril of Jerusalem, who speaks of the bread and wine becoming the body and blood of Christ, and 'no longer mere bread'. In the 5th century the development is complete, and the Epiklesis, as a definite prayer that the Holy Spirit may make the elements become the body and blood of Christ, is henceforth a feature of the Byzantine liturgies.

Between the 2nd and the 4th century, of course, the rite developed; habits tended to become ceremonies, and custom to define more closely the limits within which the celebrant was to offer prayer. Ornaments also increased, and the churches which Constantine built early in the 4th century were immensely rich—with dozens of gold chalices gemmed with emeralds, jacinths, and pearls; and patens, flagons, and pitchers of gold and silver. Lamps were hung round the altar, lamps and chandeliers elsewhere; in the Lateran basilica 130 lights hung from the ciborium, and Fleury has calculated that the number of separate lights in the whole church was 8,730, while the *Liber Pontificalis* records among other things that Constantine gave to the Lateran ninety minor chalices of gold and silver, as well as seven patens of gold and sixteen of silver, each weighing thirty pounds!

We can get an idea of the ceremonial about this time or somewhat later from the so-called *Canons of Hippolytus*; though unfortunately the book bearing this name is not of the time of Hippolytus, but full of matter belonging to the 4th, 5th, or even the 6th century, and the evidence of earlier kindred documents is inconclusive. We can therefore only say that about the 4th or 5th century the bishop, presbyters, and deacons wore

white garments 'more beautiful than those of all the people, and as splendid as possible', and that the readers also wore festival garments: we also know that the garments then in common use included the dalmatic, paenula (the *phaelonen* of 2 Tim. 4: 13, called later the chasuble), and the pallium, so that the appearance of both clergy and congregation was much the same as in the picture (Fig. 66) on this page. We also learn from them that the Offertory included gifts of corn, wine, and oil, over which a thanksgiving was said: the patens, as we have seen, were of enormous size. And further that the Anaphora, or Canon (to use another later name), began, as now, with the *Sursum Corda* ('The Lord be with you. And with thy spirit. Lift up your hearts. We lift them up unto the

66. A 6TH-CENTURY BISHOP
Mosaic of St. Eclesius in dalmatic, paenula, and pallium.

Lord. Let us give thanks unto our Lord God. It is meet and right so to do'). The Words of Administration were—'This is the body of Christ. This is the blood of Christ', the communicant responding in each case *Amen*.

The following, taken from Duchesne's *Origines*, summarizes

what can be gathered about the 4th-century Syrian customs from the writings of St. Cyril of Jerusalem and St. Chrysostom, and from the so-called *Apostolical Constitutions* which are commonly dated *c.* 370:

SYRIAN DOCUMENTS *c.* 350–400

I. LITURGY OF THE CATECHUMENS

1. THE PREPARATION

Lessons.

Two Lessons are read from an ambo or pulpit, which stands near the middle of the church; another clerk then mounts the ambo and sings a Psalm. Other Lessons and Psalms follow, always ending with the Gospel, which is read by a priest or deacon, and during which all stand.

Sermons.

The priests preach, as many as wish, and after them the bishop. Their usual seats are round the apse, facing westwards, the bishop's seat in the middle immediately behind the altar, as on p. 196.

Dismissals and Litany.

Catechumens, the excommunicate, penitents, lunatics, are dismissed, the deacon (after silent prayer) saying litanies for them, and the faithful responding *Kyrie eleison.* All communicant Christians remain.

Sursum Corda ('Lift up your hearts', &c.).

Preface and Sanctus. First part of Eucharistic Prayer (now the Preface, commemorating God's nature and work in creation, and culminating in the *Sanctus* 'Holy, holy, holy', &c.).

Continuation of Eucharistic Prayer. The bishop (always in his own words) commemorates the work of God in Redemption, the life of Christ, leading to the *Narrative of the Lord's Supper* (including 'This is my body', &c.), and followed by the *Anamnesis* or commemoration of the Passion, Resurrection, and Ascension.

The Epiklesis. He prays that the Holy Spirit will make the bread and wine the body and blood of Christ, the spiritual nourishment of the faithful, and thus performs the Consecration.

Intercession. The Eucharistic Prayer concludes with prayer for living and departed. Then the people say, *Amen.*

The Lord's Prayer, followed by a very short diaconal litany. The bishop blesses the communicants. (*The Fraction*, or breaking of the Bread, doubtless took place here, or after the *Sancta sanctis.*)

II. LITURGY OF THE FAITHFUL

2. THE OFFERTORY

Litany of Intercession and Prayer.

The deacon says the Litany for the world, the Church, the clergy, the sick, children, &c.: the people say *Kyrie eleison* after each petition. The bishop follows with a solemn prayer.

Kiss of Peace.

The bishop kisses the other clergy: the men in the congregation kiss each other, and the women kiss each other.

Oblation of the Elements.

Deacons guard the doors, and arrange the congregation, placing the children nearest the sanctuary. Others bring the bread and the chalices to the holy table and place them there, two of them waving fans to keep away flies. The bishop washes his hands, and puts on his festal robes.

3. THE EUCHARISTIC PRAYER

The Great Thanksgiving, or Anaphora.

The bishop says the grace, making the sign of the cross.

4. THE COMMUNION

The Invitation.

The bishop cries, 'Holy things for holy people' (in the old Latin Gallican rites *Sancta sanctis*). The people respond 'One only is holy, one only is the Lord . . . Glory be to God on high, and on earth peace . . . Blessed be he that cometh . . . Hosanna in the highest.'

The Communion.

All communicate; first the bishop, then the priests, deacons, subdeacons, readers, chanters, deaconesses, virgins, widows, little children, and the rest of the congregation. They take the consecrated bread in the open right hand, supported by the left, the bishop saying, 'The body of Christ'; they drink from the chalice, which is administered by the deacon, who says, 'The blood of Christ'. To each they reply *Amen.* Meanwhile the chanters sing Ps. 33. (Huge chalices stood on the altar, some weighing 12 lb.; from these must have been filled the minor 'ministerial' chalices for communicating the people.)

Thanksgiving and Dismissal.

The bishop says a prayer of thanksgiving in the name of all, and then gives the Blessing. The deacon says 'Depart in peace'.

In the 6th century we find, both in East and West, a fixed service with imposing ceremonies, still contributed on great

occasions by a number of priests and deacons who assisted
the bishop. The Eastern Liturgy has not very materially
changed since this time; and one can form some idea of what
a 6th-century Communion Service was like by attending the
Liturgy at a Greek or Russian Church.

By the 6th century also important changes were made in
the earlier part of the service, which are still conspicuous in

67. AN EARLY CHURCH ALTAR
With ornamented frontal and fair linen
From a 6th-century mosaic.

the East; the ministers entered with much pomp to the singing
of the *Monogenes* (of which a verse translation will be found in
the *English Hymnal*, no. 325); the *Trisagion* ('Holy God, Holy,
mighty, Holy and immortal, have mercy', *E. H.*, no. 737) was
sung before the Lessons; the dismissal of the catechumens had
disappeared. There had also been instituted the Great Entrance, still so striking a feature of the Eastern rite, the oblations
prepared before the service were (as they still are) carried in
procession to the holy table, while there was (as still to-day)
sung the *Cherubikon* or the *Sigesato* ('Let all mortal flesh keep
silence', *E. H.*, no. 318). The Creed was introduced into the
Eucharist at Antioch in the 5th century, and at Constantinople
in the 6th. The custom of reciting the Creed reached Spain
also in the 6th century; it spread slowly in the West and was

not adopted in Rome till 1014. In the 5th century came the reading of the Diptychs (two tables containing the names of those living and those departed to be specially prayed for) which has long disappeared from our liturgy, though indeed the practice of reading such names from a card or book is common in the Anglican Church to-day. One other feature, very conspicuous still in the East, had become customary by the 6th century—the altar was veiled during certain parts of the service. This was usually done by drawing curtains between the four pillars of the ciborium or great altar canopy (Figs. 71, 74); but in the East to-day the altar is hidden by closing the central doors of the ikonostasis or screen in front of the sanctuary.

We must now leave the Asian and Eastern Liturgies, which at the present day include the surviving Asian rites, Syrian, Persian, and the Greek and Russian Liturgies.

The Western Liturgies of to-day include the Roman, the Mozarabic, the Ambrosian (which is descended from the Gallican, and serves a million of people in the diocese and province of Milan), and the Anglican.

To follow the development in detail of the Western Liturgies would be too complicated for the reader to tolerate, or for this short history to contain. We must content ourselves here with an outline of the two great Western Liturgies in the 6th century —the Roman and the Gallican. At this time came St. Augustine of Canterbury to England bringing the Roman rite; but he had been consecrated a bishop in France according to the Gallican rite, and it was Gallican services which he found the remnant of the British Church using; and it was Gallican services which Columba and the Irish Missionaries introduced into Scotland and England.

The Roman Liturgy, as it has been for about a thousand years, can be seen—in its principal features and main outline— in any Roman missal to-day. Its original has not been traced:

all we know is that the primitive Roman service was said in
Greek and so continued until about the 4th century. The
Roman Church consisted mainly of Greek-speaking people at
first, and the reader will remember that St. Paul wrote his
Epistle to the Romans in Greek, as well as his other Epistles.

The other great Western rite, the Gallican, was fundamen-
tally different in being on the
same lines as the Eastern
rites. Some think that it was
introduced into the West
about the middle of the 4th
century; it was certainly
established in Milan before
St. Ambrose became bishop
there, and it rapidly spread
over North Italy, Gaul, Spain,
Britain, and Ireland. Others
think that the Gallican and
Eastern type was the original
Catholic type of Liturgy, and
that the Roman Liturgy was
at first exceptional. In any
case it seemed at one time as

68. THE GOURDON CHALICE
A gold cup, the earliest chalice extant.
The date is before A.D. 527.

if the whole of Christendom, outside Rome and the adjacent
territory, was destined always to use this type. But the
growing power of the Roman Church gave another turn to
the issue.

Thus the Roman Liturgy came to prevail in the West. It did
not suffer in its text during the Middle Ages as did the Divine
Service, and remains to-day much as it was in the 6th century
(it had lost the Old Testament Lesson in the 5th), sober and
primitive in tone—rather bald indeed compared with the
Eastern rites, and disfigured by some obscurities, but free from

the peculiarities of the later Medieval and modern Roman Catholic devotions.

We happen to have in *Ordo Romanus Primus* a complete description of the elaborate rites in a great Roman basilica about the year 770. The Liturgy (well described in Atchley's edition of the document) must have lasted about three hours.

69. THE GOATHLAND CHALICE
c. 1450.

70. THE JURBY CHALICE
1521–2.

The men filled one side of the nave, the women the other; the pontiff entered with many deacons, subdeacons, acolytes (i.e. clerks)—seven acolytes carried candles, a subdeacon bore a golden censer. Bishops present and priests sat in the apse with the celebrant; the other ministers stood round about the altar. (The singers would normally sit within the low marble enclosure such as we see in Figs. 71, 72.) All wore sweeping robes, paenulae (chasubles), and tunics; but the deacons took off their paenulae, to leave their arms free. Introit, *Kyries*, and *Gloria in excelsis* are sung; standing, the pontiff says the Collect. The Epistle, Gradual, &c., and Gospel are sung from an ambo (a pulpit).

At the Offertory the people bring flasks of wine which are emptied into a two-handled chalice and into bowls, and loaves which are received into bags by the acolytes. The corporal, as large as an altar cloth, has been spread by two deacons as

71. S. CLEMENTE, ROME (UPPER CHURCH)
Choir-screen and ambons of the 6th century. The ciborium, or altar canopy was set up when the Upper Church was built on the ruins of the old church in 1108.

one would spread a table-cloth to-day. Picture it all as an action in which many ministers assist, not kneeling but standing and moving about to take their different parts. For the Canon the celebrating pontiff comes down to the altar; deacons pass the paten to him, and the archdeacon holds out the chalice. During the prayer he breaks one of the loaves. After the Consecration the *Agnus* is sung, and he goes back to his throne

P

in the apse; meanwhile a curious thing happens (Is there here a last relic of the Agapè?): the chancellor and the other notaries go up and take from him the names of those to be invited to luncheon, and then distribute the invitations. Acolytes come up with sacks which the archdeacon fills with the consecrated loaves: these are taken to the apse where the higher clergy are sitting, and there are broken by them. Next these bishops and presbyters approach the throne and are communicated by the pontiff, who afterwards goes down to communicate the 'magnates', the archdeacon assisting with the chalice. For

72. S. MARIA IN COSMEDIN, ROME
Showing the presbytery and choir of a typical basilica.

the communion of the people the acolytes bring the bowls containing wine to the archdeacon, who pours into each bowl a little consecrated wine; and from these bowls the people receive through 'reeds' of gold or silver, the pontiff being now back at his seat. This over, the pontiff again comes down to the altar, and (this time facing the apse), says the post-communion collect. A deacon then says, *Ite, missa est*, the people reply, *Deo gratias*. As they go out we get a last glimpse of the seven taperers, the subdeacon with a censer, clergy of all ranks, singers, and military banner-bearers.

Broad and impressive in its sweeping dignity, this service

is unlike anything at the present day. It is still more unlike the primitive love-feast which had changed its character during the 2nd century.

It would be impossible satisfactorily to carry the history further in this little book, and we would refer those who

73. THE COMMUNION ADMINISTERED BY A BISHOP AND A DEACON

In the 13th century. (Two clerks in surplices hold the houseling cloth before the communicants.)

wish to follow the various services word for word to Brightman and to Duchesne. Suffice it to say that the Gallican rite has almost disappeared, surviving only (and that with a large Roman admixture) in the Ambrosian or Milanese rite of the North of Italy, and in the Mozarabic (see p. 21). But it had a considerable influence in the Middle Ages; and the Roman rite itself borrowed from the Gallican uses much of that ornate character which is now often regarded as specially 'Romish'.

The countries of England, Scotland, and Ireland, France and Spain, when they gave up the Gallican for the Roman Liturgy, retained some Gallican rites and ceremonies (a few of which still exist in France and in Spain); and thus there were down to the Reformation some Gallican features, akin to Eastern usage, in Latin books (such as the Sarum Missal) which were otherwise of the Roman family: various forms of the Great Entrance, for instance, and the impressive ancient custom of the benediction of the communicants by the bishop immediately before the Communion.

74. ALTAR AND CIBORIUM, *c.* A.D. 1000
High Altar of the Church of Castel, S. Elia, near Nepi.

An example (10th or 11th century) showing how the early, basilican altar was continued through the Byzantinesque period, as indeed it was in the following Romanesque period also. Many Gothic examples exist as well.

This last ceremony had become a benediction in most cases of non-communicants. During the centuries preceding the Reformation the people, for all their devotion to the Mass, were in the general habit of communicating only once a year, and a quarterly reception was uncommon even among specially devout lay folk. This grave evil was a prime cause of the reaction against the 'Mass' in the 16th

century. So the first step in England, when the 'Order of
the Communion' was inserted into the Latin service, was to
insist upon lay communion; and the succeeding Prayer Books
endeavoured to carry on the same work. Unfortunately the

75. THE COMMUNION AT A CORONATION, 1365
The King kneels to receive the Eucharist from the Archbishop, who holds
a pyx in his left hand. The crown is held by two courtiers.

Medieval habit of communicating only at Easter was so in-
grained, that the service itself came to be infrequent until the
reign of Queen Victoria.

We have seen in Chapter VI that the First Prayer Book,
while including the Order of the Communion, kept near to the
old Latin outline, but that the Canon was divided up in the
Second Book. The Scottish Liturgy was drawn more on
Eastern lines, and went through successive revisions in the same
direction; the American Liturgy followed the Scottish example.

Below we print a table of the Gallican and Roman rites in

their chief features. For the reader's convenience we have indicated by a * the parts which correspond to the present English Liturgy; while we have marked by a † parts which are still in the English service, but in a changed position; and have put ‡ by those features which in the Anglican Communion are generally supplied by hymns or anthems from one or other of the hymn books.

GALLICAN LITURGY			ROMAN LITURGY

Sixth Century

I. LITURGY OF THE CATECHUMENS			I. LITURGY OF THE CATECHUMENS
1. PREPARATION	*	*	1. PREPARATION
Preparation of the Elements	*		
Antiphon for Introit	‡		
Trisagion ('Holy God')		‡	Antiphon and Introit (psalm)
Kyrie	*	*	*Kyrie*
Canticle, *Benedictus*		†	*Gloria in Excelsis*
Collect	*	*	Collect
Lessons	*	*	**Lessons**
Old Testament Lesson			[Old Testament Lesson,
		*	dropped after 5th cent.]
		‡	Gradual (psalm)
Epistle	*	*	Epistle
Canticle, *Benedicite*; Re-sponsory *Trisagion*	‡	‡	Alleluya, or Tract (psalm)
Gospel	*	*	Gospel
Sermon	*		
Litany and Dismissal			
Litany by deacon	†		
[Dismissal a mere formula by 6th cent.]			

II. LITURGY OF THE FAITHFUL	II. LITURGY OF THE FAITHFUL

2. THE OFFERTORY   *   *   2. THE OFFERTORY

The Great Entrance. Hymn sung while the oblations are brought in, the bread in a tower-shaped vessel, and put on the altar ‡	Preparation of the Elements Chant meanwhile
	‡ Oblations put on the altar

Offertory Prayer   *   * **Offertory Prayer**

Bidding of Prayer: *Collect over oblations* *	† *Orate, fratres,* and Collect *(secreta)*
Reading of Diptychs (Commemoration of Saints and departed) *	*(Later: see below)*
Kiss of Peace, Prayer and Responsory	*(Later: see below)*

3. THE CANON   *   *   3. THE CANON

Sursum Corda, Preface, and *Sanctus* *	* *Sursum Corda,* Preface, and *Sanctus*

Eucharistic Prayer   *   * **Eucharistic Prayer**

Post-Sanctus	† *Te igitur,* Intercession, Commemoration of Saints *Hanc igitur, Quam oblationem*
Narrative of the Last Supper *	* *Qui pridie,* Narrative of the Last Supper *Unde et memores.* ('Wherefore we') *Supplices te* (prayer that the gifts may be offered on high —a weakened *Epiklesis?*)
Epiklesis, contained in the variable prayer called Post Secreta	† *Nobis quoque,* Commemoration of Saints
	† *Lord's Prayer Kiss of Peace*

GALLICAN LITURGY			ROMAN LITURGY
Fraction (breaking of the	†	†	*Fraction*
Bread)			
[In Spain the Creed here]			
Lord's Prayer		†	(*Earlier: see above*)
Commixture (particle of			Commixture
Bread placed in chalice)			

4. THE COMMUNION	*	*	4. THE COMMUNION

Sancta sanctis ('Holy things
for holy people')
Blessing of communicants

The Communion	*	*	**The Communion**
Communion (with Hymn:	‡	‡	Communion (A Psalm sung)
an Irish example is 'Draw			
nigh and take', *A. & M.*			
313, *E. H.* 307, *S. P.* 268)			
Bidding of Thanksgiving [like			'Let us pray'
'Having now received' in			
the Scottish rite]			
Post-communion (collect)	*	*	Post-communion (collect)
Dismissal	*	*	Dismissal

In comparing the above outline with our own service, four
points need special note. The *Kyries*: These in the Anglican
Liturgies are made into responsive prayers to the Ten Commandments (which may be considered as an invariable Old
Testament Lesson) or the Summary. *The Litany*: The *Kyries*
of the Latin rites are a relic of the Litany once sung in the
procession to the church. In our rite the Litany has regained
its ancient prominence as the prelude to the Liturgy itself.
The Great Entrance: The decision of the Archbishop of Canterbury in the Lincoln Case, 1890, requires the older custom of
preparing the Elements before the service, and thus restores
some form of the Great Entrance. *The Intercession and Com-*

memoration: The position of the Commemoration of departed Saints in the Church Militant prayer in all our Anglican Liturgies except the Scottish, though unlike that of the Roman or Sarum Liturgy (where the Commemoration is split up into two parts within the Canon), is the same as in the Gallican

76. CHURCH OF S. AMBROSE, MILAN
9th to 11th century.

service, where the reading of the Diptychs followed immediately on the Offertory prayer.

We are now ready to present a condensed outline of the Anglican Liturgies; from which it will be seen that our Communion Service to-day still consists of the same four principal parts, as in the time of St. Justin Martyr, and as in the succeeding ages.

THE PRESENT ANGLICAN LITURGIES

The English Liturgy, 1662, is of the Second Model, being that of the Second, Third, Fourth, and Fifth Prayer Books, i.e. those from 1552 to 1662. The Scottish and American Liturgies are of the First Model, being the type of the First Prayer Book, 1549; but the American resembles the English in the position of the Prayer for the Church, Confession, &c., in Part 2.

ENGLISH, IRISH, AND CANADIAN LITURGIES	SCOTTISH AND AMERICAN LITURGIES

I. THE PREPARATION

(Before the Liturgy: Litany, Preparation of Elements)
Lord's Prayer and Collect for Purity
Scottish omits Lord's Prayer

Lessons

(Old Testament: The Decalogue, with Kyries)
Or The Summary
Collects, Epistle, Gospel
The Creed

Sermon

2. THE OFFERTORY

The Sentences: the alms, and the bread and wine are brought to the altar

Offertory Prayer

(Church Militant Prayer [1] (i.e. Prayer over Oblations, Intercession, Commemoration)	American the same: *Scottish* defers *Scottish*: the ascription, 'Blessed be thou'
'Ye that do truly', Confession, &c.	American the same *Scottish* defers

3. THE ANAPHORA OR CANON

Sursum corda, *Preface*, and *Sanctus*

Prayer of Access [2]   Defer

Eucharistic Prayer

> A short *Anamnesis* (of the Passion and
> Sacrifice of Christ)

A personal *Epiklesis*
> Narrative from the Last Supper, with Fraction
>> The Oblation
>> The Invocation (*Epiklesis*)
>> Prayer of Oblation [3]
>>> *Scottish*: Prayer for the
>>> Church,[1] with Commem.
>>> of Saints
>> Lord's Prayer
>>> *Scottish*: The Peace

4. THE COMMUNION

Communion

>> *Scottish*: 'Ye that do truly',
>> Confession, &c.
> Prayer of Access [2]
> Communion of priest and people

Lord's Prayer
Prayer of Oblation [3] or of   *Scottish:* Short Exhortation
   Thanksgiving   Prayer of Thanksgiving

> *Gloria in Excelsis*
> (A post-Communion Collect may be added)
> The Peace and Blessing for Dismissal.

The Prayer Book, in providing for one Communion on Sundays and on Festivals, with permission to use the Collect, Epistle, and Gospel if an additional celebration is wanted, follows Catholic practice as against comparatively late developments. The Eucharist is the Lord's Day service; and, as we have noticed, even the monks of St. Benedict celebrated it only on Sundays and festivals. In the later Middle Ages there had come to be a daily celebration probably in monastic and cathedral churches, 'but not in most English parish churches', says Bishop John Wordsworth in *The Ministry of Grace* (1901).

Curiously enough, we find from Pope Innocent III that the English 18th-century custom of not having sufficiently frequent celebrations was no novelty; for he complains that some priests scarcely celebrate four times a year. Votive masses greatly increased after the Black Death; but the custom of daily cele-

77. THE COMMUNION ADMINISTERED BY A PRIEST
AND A DEACON
In the late 17th century.

bration was not established in the time of the Council of Trent, which laid down the rule 'that a bishop is to take care that priests generally are to celebrate at least on Sundays and solemn feasts, but if they have cure of souls as often as will satisfy their duty' (*Sess*. xxiii, c. 14). As for the daily Eucharist, Dr. Wordsworth says, 'The Roman Church has taken it up with extreme reluctance'; and he gives some of the reasons for this reluctance in his sixth chapter.

CHAPTER XVIII

BAPTISM, CATECHIZING, AND CONFIRMATION

WE have indicated the history of the four services in constant use, the Sacrament of the Holy Communion, its prelude—the Litany, and the two parts of the Divine Service, Mattins and Evensong. Let us now pass to the Sacrament of Initiation.

The initiation into the Christian fellowship has always consisted of two parts, Baptism and Confirmation, so closely allied in the Primitive Church that the laying on of hands was but the concluding part of the Baptismal Service—as closely allied still in the Eastern Church, where the priest anoints the babe with oil consecrated by the bishop (there being no imposition of hands) immediately after baptizing it. It is only in the Roman Catholic and Anglican Churches that the postponement of Confirmation till the age of intelligent childhood has separated from Holy Baptism the rite which completes the act of Christian initiation. In the Primitive Church the Communion followed immediately on Confirmation; and still in the East the newly baptized and confirmed babe is communicated, and Communion is habitually given to little children.

When people 'changed their minds' ('repented') and accepted Christ, the New Testament tells us, they were baptized; and the insertion in Matt. 28: 19 shows that the baptismal formula must have been introduced at an early date. We read in Acts 2: 41 that St. Peter baptized multitudes, and in Acts 8: 38 we find Philip the deacon baptizing. Acts 8: 14–17 relates how Peter and John went down to Samaria because 'they had heard that Samaria had received the word of God', to examine and sanction the admission of these non-Jews to the Church;

78. COSIN'S FONT COVER AT DURHAM

This magnificent work, a mixture of the Gothic and Renaissance styles, was erected by John Cosin when Bishop of Durham, 1660–72. His beautiful marble font was replaced in the 19th century by an imitation Norman one and is now in Pittington Church. Cosin's question to churchwardens, when Archdeacon of the East Riding, c. 1625, is typical of many other visitation articles —'Whether have you a font of stone, with a comely cover, set in the ancient usual place?'

they 'prayed for them that they might receive the Holy Spirit: for as yet he was fallen upon none of them: only they had been baptized into the name of the Lord Jesús. Then laid they their hands on them, and they received the Holy Spirit'. In other passages we read of the Holy Spirit being imparted by others, as by Ananias in Acts 9: 17, and in other ways, as in Acts 2: 4, 33, in 4: 31, and in 10: 44. But the account of St. Peter and St. John in Samaria must have had considerable effect upon the ultimate practice of the Church.

The early documents tell us a little more. In the *Didachè* (which is probably before A.D. 100) the triple formula is mentioned, and also previous instruction with fasting: a preference is expressed for the running water of a river or stream; and if the water is not deep enough for immersion, then pouring water upon the head is mentioned as sufficient.

St. Justin Martyr (*c.* A.D. 150) in his *Apology* also describes
Baptism out of doors:

'Those who are convinced of the truth of our doctrine,
and have promised to live in accordance with it, are exhorted
to prayer, fasting, and repentance for past sins; and we pray

79. BAPTISM BY IMMERSION AT THE PRESENT DAY
Land Dyaks baptized in Borneo in the presence of the Bishop of Labuan
and Sarawak.

and fast with them. Then they are led by us to a place where
there is water, and in this way they are regenerated, as we
also have been regenerated; that is to say, they receive the
bath of water in the name of God, the Father and Ruler of
all, and of our Redeemer Jesus Christ, and of the Holy Spirit.
For Christ says, "Except ye be born again, ye cannot enter
into the Kingdom of Heaven".'

Baptism was at first, of course, mainly a service for the
admission of adult converts. After the Peace of the Church,

and throughout the 4th century, great numbers of adults forsook paganism and were baptized. In the 5th, fresh races were being converted in the less central parts of the Empire; in the 6th, the conversion of our own race began. Thus there were still vast numbers of adult baptisms; and in the prolonged and elaborate ceremonies of the 6th or 7th century the service is still one of adult baptism. Undoubtedly the rite loses in impressiveness when infants are baptized, as every one knows who has witnessed the baptism of converts in the mission field. But the principle that the children of Christians shall grow up inside the Christian Church, and not as outsiders, is so important that Christendom as a whole has been content to lose the touching ceremonies of adult baptism, except on the comparatively rare occasions when it is still required. It is probable that whole families, including infants, were baptized by the Apostles, since the Baptism of Lydia and her household is mentioned (Acts 16: 15), and St. Paul mentions (1 Cor. 1: 16) that he baptized the household of Stephanas. Infant baptism was certainly held in the 2nd century to be a tradition of the Apostles.

About the year 200, Tertullian describes Baptism and Confirmation in fuller terms than Justin, speaking of the ceremonies as things long established: it is therefore certain that the sign of the cross, unction, and the giving of milk and honey are in their origin earlier than A.D. 200. Tertullian, in his epigrammatic way, sums up the whole rite of initiation:

'The flesh is washed, that the soul may be cleansed; the flesh is anointed, that the soul may be consecrated; the flesh is signed, that the soul also may be fortified; the flesh is overshadowed by the laying on of hands, that the soul may be illuminated by the Spirit; the flesh is fed with the body and blood of Christ, that the soul also may be nourished by God.'

Baptism, Tertullian says in others of his writings, is given by the bishop, and, through his authority, by priests and deacons; but in certain cases it may be conferred by lay-folk. *Preparation*: The candidate must prepare himself by prayer and fasting, and by keeping vigils. *Baptism*: It is ordinarily celebrated on Easter Even (in the night) or during the fifty days that follow. The font is blessed; the candidate solemnly renounces the devil, his pomps, and his angels [which at this time meant the renunciation of pagan ceremonies, gods, and demi-gods]; he enters the font, and is baptized in the Name of the Father, the Son, and the Holy Spirit.

80. SYMBOLIC REPRESENTATION OF BAPTISM
From the Catacomb of Callistus, 2nd century.

The dove shows that the subject is the Baptism of Christ; but there are contemporary pictures in the Catacombs of the baptism of catechumens which are exactly similar, except that there is no dove and that the minister wears the tunic or pallium instead of the loin-cloth as here. On the left is another ancient symbol of Baptism—a fisherman drawing a fish out of the sea.

Confirmation: The bishop then anoints him with consecrated oil, signs him with the cross, and lays his hands upon him, invoking the Holy Spirit. *First Communion*: Tertullian alludes to this in the same quotation; and in another place he mentions that milk and honey were given to the new communicants; this was a sign that they had reached the Promised Land, 'flowing with milk and honey'.

We can imagine with what solemnity, and with what a hush of awe, these appealing ceremonies were celebrated over men and women, who thus renounced paganism, and entered the fold where they were henceforward to live—sometimes in peril of agony and death. Careful testing and instruction were necessary before a pagan could be admitted into the Church.

Thus it was that, first of all, when any candidates presented themselves, their names were taken down and inquiries made into their characters: they were then admitted as *catechumens*, normally for a period of two or three years, though the period could be made shorter or longer. When the ages of suspicion and occasional persecution passed away and the Peace of the Church had begun, the Catechumenate was abused by many converts from paganism, who remained catechumens—such was the awe which Baptism inspired—and did not enter the font till old age or the time of their last illness. Among those who set the bad example was the Emperor Constantine himself. But there were also many earnest men, feeling their way to the new thought, who waited in their reverence till they should be less unworthy and untrained for the heavy responsibility of being a Christian. St. Martin of Tours, for instance, born about the time of Constantine's death, and destined to be one of the wisest of bishops, was only a catechumen when as a young soldier he gave his cloak to the beggar.

We know that in the 4th century the candidate was admitted to the Catechumenate with much ceremony, which included the exsufflation, or breathing upon him, the signing with the cross, in Rome the placing of a grain of salt in his mouth, in Spain a preliminary unction. The preparation of the catechumens through Lent included solemn visits to the church. These 'scrutinies' were seven in the Rome of the 7th century, with exorcisms and prayer at each (the whole world both Christian and pagan was obsessed with the idea that there were evil spirits in everything). At the third visit took place 'the delivery of the Christian Law'—the four Gospels being laid on the altar, read from and explained—the delivery of the Creed, and of the Lord's Prayer.

This practice, changed to less formal catechizing, continued through the Middle Ages; and we have it still in our Church

Catechism, which is an instruction to be delivered in church in preparation for Confirmation, on these same subjects—the Creed, the Christian Law (for the Decalogue is in the Catechism made Christian by the Duty to God and the Duty to our Neighbour), the Lord's Prayer. The Church Catechism is in fact an instruction, admirably condensed, on these three things, prefixed by the teaching of the Baptismal Vow, and followed by the appendix on the Sacraments.

81. A BAPTISTERY, RAVENNA. 5TH CENTURY
With large 5th-century font for immersion.

Thus it was then that, as the Empire became Christian, and persons were increasingly admitted into the Church in infancy, the Catechumenate changed its character, and became the catechizing of children after their Baptism, and often after their Confirmation as well.

But the initiatory rite was still celebrated with great magnificence, and infants were treated as if they were adults, their part being taken by deputy—by godparents, in fact. Here, then, again, in the replies made by the sponsors at our service, we have a reminder of the days when Europe was in process of conversion from paganism to Christianity.

ABOUT THE 4TH CENTURY

A good deal can be put together from passages in various writers and a coherent account of the baptismal service given, such as has been written by Brightman in Swete's *Early History of the Church and the Ministry*, of which we give here a summary.

1. *The Baptism*

Nightfall. Ante-Communion Service, prolonged; lessons, hymns, and a sermon, till cock-crow. Then the ministers and catechumens go to the baptistery: the bishop prays over the water, and consecrates two kinds of oil. Then, 1. The Renunciation: 'I renounce thee, Satan, and all thy works', &c., the form varying but being in effect a comprehensive repudiation of paganism. 2. The Exorcism, an oil of exorcism being used in some places. 3. The Confession of Faith. Standing in the font with a deacon, each candidate says a short summary of the Creed. 4. The Act of Baptism. Standing by the font, the bishop or presbyter asks, 'Dost thou believe in God the Father Almighty?', the candidate answers, 'I believe', and the bishop baptizes him once; and so on with the second and third parts of the Creed. In Rome there was for centuries no other baptismal formula besides these three questions, though elsewhere a formula like ours was used as the bishop poured the water over the candidate or plunged him in it.

2. *Confirmation*

They all return to the church; and the bishop lays his hand on each neophyte with a prayer for grace. He then pours oil on the head of each, signs him on the brow, and kisses him.

Unction was not used in the African Church, but was already more prominent than the laying on of hands in the East.

3. *Communion*

The Communion Service is now resumed; and at the Offertory the neophytes give their oblations of bread. Wine, water, and milk and honey are also offered. At the Great Thanksgiving or Eucharistic Prayer cups of water and of milk and honey are on the table as well as the bread and wine. Each neophyte is then communicated as follows: first, the bishop breaks the consecrated bread and gives a portion to each, saying, 'The heavenly bread in Christ Jesus', and the neophyte answers, 'Amen'. Then the presbyters or deacons follow with the three chalices, and administer successively the water (as a symbol of baptism), the milk and honey (as a symbol of the Promised Land after the Jordan of baptism), and lastly the wine, with the words, 'In God the Father Almighty', each communicant again answering 'Amen', 'And the Lord Jesus Christ, and the Holy Spirit, and the holy Church', the answer again being 'Amen'.

7TH AND 8TH CENTURIES

Here is a summary of the rites three or four centuries later from the longer account which Duchesne has gathered together out of three Roman books. Although the baptism of grown-up people is now exceptional, the service used is still that for adults.

Baptism

Maundy Thursday. A vase of oil and a vase of chrism (oil perfumed with balm) are consecrated towards the end of the Canon. The people add little vials of oil for their personal use in the anointing of the sick.

Easter Even. (Afternoon or morning.) The last exorcism. The Effeta, or touching of the lips and ears. Unction on the breast and back. The candidates renounce Satan (turning to the West in the Oriental Churches) and recite the Creed (turning to the East). They depart, after prayer.

Easter Even. (The night service.) The Easter Vigil with long Lessons from the Old Testament interspersed with Psalms and Canticles.

The bishop and his clergy go, in a litany-procession with lights and incense, to the baptistery. (In the midst of the tank-like font of the great Roman baptistery of St. John Lateran was a large porphyry candelabrum with a golden lamp of perfumed oil: there were silver statues of Christ and St. John Baptist, with the Lamb of God in the midst, and under it a fountain of water that fell into the font; jets of water also sprang from seven stags' heads round the font.) As the Litany ceases, prayers are said, and the bishop signs the water: two ministers then plunge lighted tapers into the water, and the bishop pours chrism on it in the form of a cross, stirring it with his hand.

The candidates then take off their clothes in two adjoining vestries. The archdeacon presents them to the bishop, and they make a threefold profession of faith. The bishop, with priests and deacons (all wearing long linen tunics), enters the water with the candidates; he pours water over their heads, saying, 'I baptize thee in the name of the Father, and of the Son, and of the Holy Spirit'.

Confirmation

They go into a church or chapel (at St. John Lateran, the Chapel of the Cross, behind the baptistery) for the Consignation or signing. The bishop anoints their heads with chrism. They put on white robes, assisted by their godfathers and godmothers. (In the Gallican and Celtic rites the bishop now girds himself and washes the feet of the newly baptized.) The bishop invokes the Holy Spirit and crosses the forehead of each neophyte with his thumb moistened with the chrism, saying to each one, 'In the name of the Father, and of the Son, and of the Holy Spirit.

82. BAPTISM IN THE 14TH CENTURY
The parson wears an apparelled albe without a stole, and (following the Sarum and York Manuals) holds the babe in his arms. From an English manuscript.

Peace to thee.' (In the Eastern Churches the neophytes then turn to the East and recite the Lord's Prayer.)

First Communion

During the Baptism and Confirmation the choir have sung Litanies in the Church. A procession now enters from the baptistery; the bishop prostrates himself before the altar, stands, and intones the *Gloria in Excelsis*, thus beginning the first Eucharist of Easter Day. It is still night. At this service the neophytes make their first Communion, standing before the altar in their white robes. Afterwards they drink water and milk and honey, which have been blessed during the Canon. (This ceremony was given up at Rome about the time of Gregory the Great. It is still retained in the Coptic Church.) Then with the dawn comes Easter Day.

83. BAPTISM IN THE 15TH CENTURY

The priest, wearing a surplice without a stole, holds the babe over the font. A clerk behind him holds the manual open. A man and two women are also present.

From the font at Sloley, Norfolk.

During the Octave of Easter the neophytes wear their white robes and go to church every day.

Most of these imposing ceremonies have been preserved in a more or less attenuated form up to the present time, in one part or other of the Church; but as the need of adult baptism decreased and multitudes of infants all over Christendom had to be baptized, the rites changed both in significance and in character. The times for the rite were increased, Whitsuntide being added first in the West, the Epiphany and Christmas in the East; priests, who had at first merely assisted the bishop, carried out the rites on these great occasions in his presence, the blessing of the oil of Confirmation being, however, always reserved to him; then, as necessity required, they administered baptism without him on other Holy-days (the first Baptismal Rubric of the Prayer Book still gives 'Sundays and other Holydays' as the proper occasions for this Sacrament). In the East

84. A BISHOP ON A JOURNEY, 1520

He rides a mule, and wears a hood and chimere over his rochet. Three clerks accompany him on mules, and three precede him on foot.

they administer Communion also to the newly baptized, the bishop's part consisting only in the annual consecration of the chrism.

But in the West, as the bishop's presence was still required, the newly baptized had to wait till the occasion of an episcopal visit, and often had to wait a long time. Hence children were sometimes quite old before the bishop came their way and confirmed them, wearing his rochet and hood or chimere, and often performing the short rite on horseback, in the Middle Ages (it was noted of St. Hugh of Lincoln that once he dismounted for a confirmation with as much reverence as if he

had been in his cathedral); and thus the custom of infant
Confirmation and Communion slowly and gradually died out.
At the last revision in 1661 advantage was taken of this to make
Confirmation the occasion for a public renewal of the baptismal

85. CONFIRMATION OF INFANTS IN
THE 15TH CENTURY

The bishop, wearing a rochet and hood, with
a cap on his head, confirms by unction an infant
held by a woman on his right. On his left a
clerk holds the casket containing the oil: he
seems also to be wearing a rochet

*This mutilated panel is from the font at East
Dereham, Norfolk.   The period is that of
Edward IV*

vows, when children had
reached years of discretion;
but the Reformers intended
them to be still rather young
at the time of their Confirmation and First Communion,
and, until the 19th century,
they were sometimes under
ten, and seldom more than
a year or two older.

Medieval England, while
retaining in a shrunken form
most of the ceremonies of
the ancient Roman Church,
had also some Gallican customs, notably the presentation of a lighted candle to
the babe. The Blessing of the
Font had become a separate
service, performed on Easter
Even and the Vigil of Pentecost, when the water was re-
newed and hallowed, whether there were any children to be
then baptized or not: this solemn benediction was indeed the
only one of the ancient rites that retained anything like the
ancient splendour. The baptism itself was a service probably
little more imposing in its common administration than the
hurried rite which one witnesses to-day in Italy or France.

The First English Prayer Book brought back into its proper

86. BAPTISM AND CONFIRMATION IN THE 15TH CENTURY

Two scenes from the picture of the Seven Sacraments by Rogier van der Weyden, Antwerp, c. 1450.

A priest in long surplice and stole is anointing the babe as part of the baptismal act. Behind, a bishop confirms by anointing, while a minister binds a napkin round the head of another candidate who has already been anointed.

prominence the actual baptizing of the infant, which in the Sarum rite had been smothered up among ceremonies that had long lost most of their meaning. The Blessing of the Font was still a separate service, and was ordered to be done once a month. The preparatory part of the service (a relic of the Catechumenate) still took place at the church-door, near which the font always stood in the Middle Ages, as it is bound by law to do still; the babe was named, signed on the forehead and breast, and exorcised. After the Gospel, the priest and people said the Lord's Prayer and Creed, and then all went to the font, where the service proceeded much as now. After the Baptism, the child was anointed, and clad in the white robe (called the chrisom).

In the Second Prayer Book the prayers for Blessing the Font (taken by Cranmer in 1549 from the Gallican Mozarabic Missal) were placed immediately before the baptism. The surviving relic of the Catechumenate was further reduced by the omission of the exorcism and Creed, and the transference of the signing with the Cross and of the Lord's Prayer to their present place after the baptizing. The service was made to begin at the font itself, and thus the little procession from the church-door was lost, with its seemly words, 'The Lord vouchsafe to receive you into his holy household, and to keep and govern you alway in the same, that you may have everlasting life'. The unction and white robe were omitted. At the last Revision in 1662, the blessing of the font was made clearer by the insertion of the sentence 'Sanctify this Water to the mystical washing away of sin', and the words 'of Infants' were added to the title, because the new service for Adults was then added to the Prayer Book, which thus touched hands with the earliest baptismal rites. At this time also, the Catechism was taken out of the Confirmation service and printed separately.

An idea has grown up in recent years which has done not

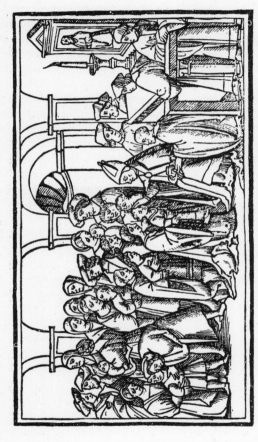

87. A BISHOP CONFIRMING CHILDREN, 1520

The Bishop, in his rochet, cope, and mitre, is signing the forehead of a child, who is held up by a kneeling sponsor. By him kneels a clerk in surplice, holding a dish containing the oil-stock. By the altar are four clergymen in surplices and caps.

a little harm: it is the notion that there is one proper and correct way of performing each of the services of the Church, and that if everything is not carried out according to some imagined standard, a great offence is done against what is supposed to be Catholic order. It is, of course, true that in each Church the duty of the clergy is to obey the rubrics of that Church and to follow its lawful customs; and it is equally true that when they prefer their own private judgment, they do so to the great detriment of the services—as happened, for example, during the Georgian era, when children were baptized in the drawing-rooms of private houses, or from small basins put in the font. But the preceding chapters of this little book will have at least made it clear that there is no one and only way of performing any rite of the Church; and of nothing is this more true than of the many and changing rites and ceremonies which have gathered round the two acts of the Christian initiation.

CHAPTER XIX
THE OCCASIONAL SERVICES

W E will conclude this history with an historical summary of those services which are for special occasions in a Christian's life, and which were formerly an application of the Holy Communion to those occasions. They were all still thus connected in the First Prayer Book; but the Second Book made a difference in the case of the Burial Service, which is therefore in the present English Prayer Book without a special Epistle and Gospel, though these are found in the present American, Scottish, and Canadian Books and in the South African Occasional Offices.

THE SOLEMNIZATION OF MATRIMONY

This, like most of the Occasional Services, is taken from the Sarum Manual. It has also a peculiar interest in carrying on some innocent pagan ceremonies. The reason of this is that, in the early Church, Christians naturally followed the legal customs of the Roman Empire; and all they could do was to substitute a Christian benediction for the specifically heathen rites, and, instead of a sacrifice to idols, to offer the Christian memorial of the Eucharist. Marriage was, before Christianity, and is still, a natural compact, of which the man and the woman themselves are the ministers: this compact, made before witnesses, constitutes a marriage when it is consummated, but to it the Church has added, from early times, the blessing of the bride and bridegroom and their communion. Thus our present service, which is the espousal and benediction, ends with the rubric that 'It is convenient [i.e. fitting] that the new-married persons should receive the holy Communion at the time of their Marriage, or at the first opportunity after their Marriage'.

Even after the 6th century, the Christian solemnization of matrimony still in many places consisted merely of prayers inserted in the Communion service, a veil being held over the man and woman during one of the prayers. This ancient nuptial veil was still common in France and Spain in the 19th century, though modern Ultramontanism has caused it to disappear. The other veil, the bride's, flame-coloured in pagan times, is still with us, though its colour is now white.

88. MARRIAGE IN THE 15TH CENTURY
The parson, wearing apparelled amice, albe, and crossed stole (and for the artist's purpose made of giant proportions), joins the hands of the pair. A clerk holds the book.

From the font panel at Sloley, Norfolk.

The old civil ceremonies of paganism thus went on side by side with the primitive nuptial service; and as paganism disappeared, they came to be included in the Christian books. In ancient Rome these were: *The Betrothal*: The contracts were signed, presents were given (as a token of the marriage settlement), the bride and bridegroom kissed, the ring was given, and hands were joined. *The Wedding*: The bride and bridegroom (the bride veiled, and both wearing crowns and the nuptial attire) offered sacrifices, and partook of the sacrificial cake made by the Vestal Virgins.

We know from the mention of them by Tertullian that in

the year 200, the kiss, and the joining of hands, the crown, and the veil were used, while for the sacrifices and the sacrificial meal the Oblation (as he calls it) had been substituted, the mystical meal of the Communion. The ring must also have continued in use.

The reader will at once notice that all these things are still with us, even to the kiss, though this is now an unauthorized ceremony, usually performed in the chancel or vestry by the married couple, who do not often know that they are carrying out a ceremony of the Early Church. The bride in England still wears a crown (but this is less common in America); and, though it is now with us a wreath of flowers, in some Western countries metal crowns are still used (as they were in Medieval England); and in the East both the man and the woman wear large diadems of metal, and the whole marriage ceremony is called the Crowning.

In the Middle Ages the service continued much the same, with variations in different places. It consisted of two main parts—(1) the Espousal at the church-door or chancel-step, when the man and woman plighted their troth, the ring was given, and the couple were blessed; (2) the Nuptial Mass, with its solemn nuptial benediction before the Communion. During the Liturgy the pair knelt first on the south of the sanctuary, and then at the altar-step for the *Sanctus*, while the nuptial veil was held over them till the *Agnus*—the votive Mass of the Trinity being usually taken, with some variations. The words 'and obey' are omitted from the American and Scottish Books, but retained in the Irish and Canadian; in England advantage is often taken of their omission from the Deposited Book, which made this and many other improvements in the Occasional Services. These words are a late Medieval addition of about the 14th century, when the words 'obeye to him' first appear in the English rite, and similar words in some German uses. In most Christian rites, the questions put to and the promises made by both parties are identical: in some rites—e.g. all over the East, both parties receive rings. Another controverted

89. A MARRIAGE, 1745

The priest, in surplice and bands, holding the prayer book,
is assisted by a clerk in gown and bands.

From the picture in the Tate Gallery, London, by Joseph Highmore
(1692–1780); entitled 'Pamela is Married'.

feature, the opening address, appears first in 1549. The impressive form 'Those whom God hath joined' (of Lutheran origin, though it appears also in the rites of Soissons and Milan) was also introduced in the First Book. The third part of the Solemnization of Holy Matrimony, the Communion, may now be deferred till a later day. Until it was relaxed in 1662, the rubric ordered that 'The new married persons (the same day of their marriage) must receive the holy Communion'.

ORDER FOR THE VISITATION
OF THE SICK

In the Early Church the sick were visited for Communion, for prayer, and for unction or the laying on of hands. Our present order follows closely the lines of the *Visitatio Infirmorum* in the Sarum Manual, with two important exceptions: 1. The rite of unction was left out of the Second Prayer Book. It has, however, been restored, together with the Laying on of Hands, in the American and Scottish Books; and the Deposited Book in England would have restored the Laying on of Hands. 2. Taking the Sacrament to the sick, a custom that is mentioned by Justin Martyr (pp. 194–5), was omitted at the same time. On the other hand, a special form for celebrating the Eucharistic service in the sick-room had been inserted in the First Prayer Book: in the Second Book this was altered, and no provision made for shortening the full service; but in 1662 this impracticable defect was made good. Communicating

90. A PRIEST CATECHIZING, 1689
Frontispiece to *The Catechumen*, licensed 1689. (He wears his cassock and full-sleeved gown. In the background is sketched an altar with chalice and flagon thereon.)

the sick and infirm with the reserved Sacrament (in both kinds) was provided for in the Deposited Book of 1928, amid much controversy. It was traditional in Scotland, even in the days when the surplice had not been revived there, and has been the long-standing custom in most of the old native Scottish congregations; the anointing of the sick was also revived by some Scottish bishops in the 18th century, and has there continued since. This is confirmed in the Scottish Prayer Book of 1929. The Scottish and Irish Books and the English Deposited Book conveniently divide the Order into sections.

THE ORDER FOR THE BURIAL OF THE DEAD

We know that as far back as evidence can be found on the customs of the Primitive Church—that is, in the paintings on the walls of the Catacombs from about the year 100—the bodies of Christians were laid to rest with prayer and the meal of fellowship; and that afterwards memorial services for the departed were held, at which the Agapè or Communion was celebrated. The many chapels scattered among these vast subterranean corridors were not, as used to be supposed, concealed places for ordinary worship: they were, on the contrary, open to public knowledge and protected by the pagan authorities (since ancient Roman law had profound respect for everything connected with the dead); and they were made for memorial services, and not for the normal worship of the Church, which indeed required far larger places.

One unique relic of the Agapè still exists, the hall actually built in the 1st century for the love-feast. It consists of a room with a large *triclinium* showing traces of its stone bench, a smaller room, a kitchen (where wine-jars and utensils were unearthed), a well and cistern: this room forms the vestibule to the Catacomb of St. Domitilla, only in part underground, and it originally had an ornamental façade upon the high road.

91. FUNERAL IN A MONASTIC CHURCH

From an early 16th-century Flemish Book of Hours.

The hearse stands between two lights on the rush-strewn floor of the choir. Behind, under a double triptych (the lower wings closed) is the high altar vested in a bright red frontal, the carpet on the steps is pale blue, and the curtains are bright green, as are the riddels, the posts of which are surmounted by angels. A gospel lectern in the form of a pelican stands on a step at the north side of the presbytery.

Chapels for service within the Catacombs are many in number: a restoration of a somewhat late (4th century) example from the Catacomb of Callistus is given on p. 196.

The early Sacramentaries, which are the earliest of extant service books, give the whole cycle of rites for the sick, the dying, and the departed; and from these come the Medieval services. As early as A.D. 688 we find our own Anglo-Saxon customs, borrowed from those of Old Rome, in a description of that Archbishop Theodore to whom England owes so much. The dead, he says, were taken by monks or religious men to the church, where the Eucharist was celebrated, and then they were taken with chanting to their graves, to be there buried with prayer for them.

In the Middle Ages a special form of the Divine Service for the departed grew up, and from this we have the word 'dirge': the Mattins (with Lauds) was called the *Dirige* or Dirge, from the words of the opening Antiphon, 'Dirige Domine Deus meus in conspectu tuo viam meam' (from Ps. 5: 8, correctly rendered in the Prayer Book and in the Revised Version, 'Make thy way plain before my face'); the Evensong, for the same reason, was called the *Placebo*, the opening Antiphon being 'Placebo Domino in regione vivorum' (from Ps. 116: 9, 'I will walk before the Lord in the land of the living'). These were extensively used in a general way, as well as at funerals.

The long exercise of prayer began at the sick-bed, with psalms and litanies ending with petitions that God would receive his servant in his goodly habitation of light. After death, the Commendation was said, a service of Antiphons, Psalms, and Collects.

The body, covered with a pall of bright colours, was carried to church with the singing of psalms, and placed in the standing frame of wood or iron, called the hearse, surrounded by tapers (as on p. 245). The mourners wore black cloaks and hoods (a

92. A BURIAL IN THE 15TH CENTURY

(The body is being carried out of the church by men in mourners' cloaks and hoods, preceded by one carrying a lighted torch. A priest in surplice and cope approaches the grave preceded by a boy carrying the holy water vat and sprinkler, and another in a surplice carrying a processional crucifix; he is followed by two clerks, one wearing a winged rochet, and the other a high cap with his surplice or rochet. A typical wooden grave-cross will be noticed in front of the kneeling woman on the left.

custom which survived into the 19th century). Then the *Placebo* and Dirge were said or sung, leading up to the Requiem Mass, so-called from the Introit which opens the service, 'Requiem aeternam dona eis, Domine, et lux perpetua luceat eis' ('Rest eternal grant to them, O Lord, and may light perpetual shine upon them'). There was now a second and shorter Commendation, and the hearse was censed and sprinkled. Then the burial service itself began. After an antiphon, *Kyrie*, and prayers, the body was carried to the grave, while 'When Israel came out of Egypt' was sung, followed, if the procession was long, by the psalm, 'Unto thee, O Lord, will I lift up my soul'.

The grave was then blessed, sprinkled, and censed, and the body laid to rest, while the company sang the psalm, 'Like as the hart desireth the water-brooks: so longeth my soul after thee, O God', thus joining in spirit, as throughout all the services, with their departed friend. After the psalm, 'Lord, remember David', the body was sprinkled with holy water, and the priest scattered earth on it in the form of a cross with a form beginning, 'I commend thy soul to God'. Then were more prayers, and the three triumphant psalms of Lauds—'O praise the Lord of heaven', 'O sing unto the Lord a new song', and 'O praise God in his holiness'; there followed the *Benedictus* (the Antiphon to which, 'I am the Resurrection and the Life', we still retain), and the penitential *Miserere*, with a few last prayers of love and hope. Afterwards, and especially on the 'month's mind' and the anniversary, the *Placebo* and Dirge were said, and Eucharists celebrated. Thus, in the wonderful beauty of their churches, and in the churchyards, unchilled by the gleam of polished gravestones and glass flowers, did our forefathers carry out the last, offices they could render to their friends, with ancient rites of comfort and cheer and help.

There was another side to all this, and the reaction at the Reformation was extreme. We cannot here discuss all the causes. Certain it is that a morbid religion of fear had grown up at the close of the Middle Ages after the Black Death, to which the outward ceremonial of Roman Catholic countries abroad still bears witness with its decorations of skulls and cross-bones. Certain it is that, in the place of the paradise of flowers, which the pictures in the Catacombs always portray, and of which the first Latin Christian poet, Prudentius, sings, there had grown up a 'Romish doctrine concerning Purgatory', which made it a place of fire, differing from that of Hell only in not being everlasting: and with this there came a feverish desire for innumerable Masses, such as only the rich could afford, which is luridly illustrated in the Will of Henry VIII. Some reaction was inevitable. Unfortunately it took at first in most men's minds the form of Calvinism, which is really Augustinianism and is—in the literal sense of the word—*infinitely* worse than even the Medieval doctrine concerning Purgatory. It was no use praying for the damned.

Amid the hideous funeral customs of the Georgian era, men thought with relief of the Prayer Book Burial Service, and called it exquisite and incomparable. It does indeed merit much praise; but it is perhaps, as it stands in the English Book of 1662, the least satisfactory of the services.

In the First Prayer Book Cranmer undertook the simplifica-tion of the Medieval rites, which were over-long by virtue of their many repetitions; and he produced one of his best pieces of work in the new Order for the Burial of the Dead, which is a real simplification, at once primitive and traditional, consisting as it does of the four essential parts of the old rite—(1) The Procession; (2) The Burial; (3) The Office of the Dead, to be said either after or before the Burial; (4) The Eucharist. The Second Book produced a mere confusion, left no psalms at all, and no Eucharist, and did not so much as provide that any part of the service should be said in Church. But even this was too much for the Puritans, who actually had no service whatever. When in the 18th century poor Jamie Fleeman 'the Laird of Udny's Fool' was wounded and dying, he managed to crawl over the hills of East Aberdeenshire to Longside, where he knew

93. THE HIGH ALTAR OF WESTMINSTER ABBEY
Arranged for a Funeral or Memorial Service

there was an Episcopal church; and when they found him, he said, 'Dinna bury me like a beast!'—alluding to what was the universal Presbyterian practice until recent times. The Fifth Book restored something of what the Second had thrown away, but the psalms it gave us were new; and the second Antiphon, being conformed to the Authorized Version of the Bible, introduced the horrid reference to worms, which we might have been spared at such a time, and which mercifully is untrue in fact, as well as a mistranslation. The translators of the Authorized

Version seem to have borrowed the worms from the Geneva Bible; for they are not in the original Hebrew, nor in the Vulgate.

The American and other Anglican churches have, however, made many improvements; and the English Church itself has never been confined to the Burial Service of 1662. The Latin Prayer Book of 1560 gave us with authority a Collect, Epistle, and Gospel for a Eucharist, and a Commendation Service for founders and benefactors; and the Elizabethan Primer gave us both the *Placebo* and the Dirge. The Canons of 1604 provide, with the authority of Convocation, the beautiful commemoration of the departed in the Bidding Prayer. Many commemorative services have been put forth since, including those (drawn up by the Archbishops and issued by the King in Council) for Queen Victoria and King Edward VII, the latter of which contains a Collect, Epistle, and Gospel for the Eucharist. Queen Victoria herself did much to restore a better memory of the dead; and our 20th-century hymnals have supplied what was missing in the earlier hymn-books. Very good arrangements of funeral and memorial services are given in the Deposited Book of 1928. A special service for the burial of a child is a modern improvement in all our later Anglican Books: Canada, 1918; Ireland, 1926; America, 1929; Scotland, 1929; South Africa, 1930.

THE CHURCHING OF WOMEN

This short service is very like that in the Sarum Manual; and the rite itself is mentioned in the 6th century by St. Augustine of Canterbury. The principal changes are: The addition of the opening sentence; the change of psalms (which were 121 and 128 in the Sarum rite, 121 in the First and Second Prayer Books, and now 116 and 127—all being appropriate in various ways); the addition, in the last revision, of the words, 'We give

thee humble thanks', to emphasize the fact that the service is
one of thanksgiving. The words, 'decently apparelled', in the
first rubric, were also added in 1662, but they only carry on
the old usage; for they were inserted to ensure the woman
wearing the customary white veil, which the Puritans had tried
to give up, and which had been enforced by law (although there
was then no rubric) in the reigns of James I and Charles I. The
disregard of this rule has in modern times lessened the beauty
of the service, which needs the emphasis of a simple ceremonial,
such as the white veil (the carrying of a light, perhaps, by the
woman), and her being supported by two matrons—customs
which seem to have been all continued after the Reformation.
The English Deposited Book of 1928 makes the excellent
suggestion that the woman shall be accompanied by her hus-
band: like the Scottish and South African forms, it adds a
prayer for both parents in their educational capacity. In the
American Book the Woman's Thanksgiving may be said by
itself at any service at which she is present, and the Service
itself is left to the discretion of the Minister.

A COMMINATION

The Commination is a substitute for the Reconciliation of
Penitents on Ash Wednesday, which is first described in the
Gelasian Sacramentary of the 7th or 8th century. The 51st
Psalm, the suffrages, and the two collects following, are taken
from the Medieval form, which dates from about the 12th
century, and applied not to penitents specially, but to all the
faithful, upon whose heads ashes were placed, before the Reformation. The rest, which forms the opening part of the Commination, was added in the First Prayer Book. The service
is appointed to be said immediately after the Litany, that is
to say, before the Ash Wednesday Communion.

The long Address, magnificent as a piece of English, has been dropped in the American and Scottish Books: in the Deposited Book a new Address was given at the end of the book; but this also, though finely written, is not very suitable for present-day needs. The curses, derived from the Greater Excommunication of the Sarum Manual, have been modified in a not altogether successful manner by the Canadian Church. The Sentences substituted in the Irish Prayer Book are a very great improvement. In the Scottish Book the Decalogue is substituted; and in the American the whole section is omitted, the service beginning with the 51st Psalm, from which the concluding verse is rightly omitted.

94. THE COMMINATION
From a Print by Hollar, c. 1670.
The priest kneels in his cassock and surplice at the Litany-desk, between the congregation and the altar; a book lies on the altar eastward.

FORMS OF PRAYER TO BE USED AT SEA

These were added in the last English Revision of 1662, and are not included in the American or Scottish Books. They are not complete services, but additions to the ordinary offices of the Prayer Book.

FORM FOR THE CONSECRATION OF A CHURCH, FOR THE INSTITUTION OF A MINISTER, AND OTHER FORMS

Several useful Forms have been added by the Anglican Churches. In the *American Prayer Book* are (1) a Form for

95. ST. NICHOLAS, BURNAGE, MANCHESTER

The Chapel is raised above the vestries and is separated from the sanctuary by the large wrought-iron grill

(*N. F. Cachemaille-Day, architect*)

the Consecration of a Church or Chapel, (2) for the Institution of Ministers, and (3) a Form of Family Prayer, as well as the addition to the Catechism of three Offices of Instruction in which it is expanded. The *Canadian Book* adds to the first three of these a Form for the Consecration of a Churchyard or Cemetery, a Form of Service for Dominion Day and other Occasions, a Service for Children, others for Missions, for Harvest Thanksgiving, and for the Laying of a Foundation Stone. The *Irish Book*, in addition to the services for an Institution, and for the Consecration of a Church and of a Churchyard, gives a service for the first Sunday on which a Minister officiates in a Church. The *Scottish Book*—apart from its containing the Scottish Liturgy as well as the English— is content with one addition, that of Compline, a service for use before going to bed, which in its origin is later than, as it is inferior to, the great choir services. The *South African* additional services include a Form of Confession and Absolution, and provide for the needs of a Province that contains many races by forms for Reception into the Congregation, for the Admission of Catechumens, and for the Blessing of a Civil Marriage.

CHAPTER XX

THE ORDINAL

IN the Greek Testament the word *Diakonos* (deacon) means a minister or servant, *Presbyteros* (presbyter, shortened in English to 'priest') an elder, and *Episcopos* (shortened in English to 'bishop') an overseer. At first, and in St. Paul's earlier Epistles (e.g. 1 Cor. 12: 28), the place of honour is held by Apostles, Prophets, and Teachers; and the Church at Antioch was managed by prophets and teachers, as we read in Acts 13: 1. On one occasion seven men were elected to act as almoners, and in Acts 6 the word *diakonia* is applied to their ministry. They were admitted by prayer and the laying on of hands; as were also Paul and Barnabas when they were sent forth on their mission by the prophets and teachers who managed affairs at Antioch; but prayer and the imposition of hands are not in the New Testament peculiar to ordination. On the return visit of their first missionary journey Paul and Barnabas 'appointed for them elders (*presbyteroi*) in every church' (Acts 14: 23). In his address to those whom St. Luke calls the 'elders' of Ephesus (Acts 20: 17) St. Paul adjures them solemnly as overseers ('bishops'): there were, therefore, at Ephesus overseers who could be called elders; but it does not follow that all elders could be called overseers. In the later Epistle to the Philippians (1: 1) St. Paul singles out for salutation the overseers and ministers. Gradually the overseers, elders, and ministers (in modern language, 'bishops, priests, and deacons,') rose into the place of honour at first held by apostles, prophets, and teachers. In the Epistles to Timothy and Titus, which probably in their present form are not later than A.D. 110, overseers and elders are mentioned, and also ministers and 'women' who were probably deaconesses; and stress is laid upon the 'laying on of hands of the presbytery' (1 Tim. 4: 14), and to 'the gift of God which is in thee through the laying on of my hands' (2 Tim. 1: 6). In the 2nd century some churches seem to have been managed by ' overseers ', some by presbyters; and the Church of

96. 'TRADITION' OR DELIVERY OF A GOSPEL BOOK TO A NEWLY-CONSECRATED BISHOP, 1520

The bishop kneels in his chasuble. Behind him are four priests in surplices. Behind the three consecrating bishops are the altar and reredos.

Rome, curiously enough, by a committee of presbyters in what we should now call the Presbyterian way. In the end, however, the Episcopal system became universal, doubtless because it was found to work better than other methods.

Third- and fourth-century documents show that the laying on of hands with appropriate prayer was used for bishops, priests, and deacons. Mention is also made of minor orders— subdeacons and readers; but these were not ordained by the imposition of hands in the West, nor as yet generally in the

East. In the Old Roman services of the 6th, 7th, and 8th centuries, ordination still consisted entirely of prayer, accompanied by the imposition of hands. These two things, then, were regarded as the essential features of the rite.

There were in Rome at this time, and had been for three centuries, five minor orders of ministers (making eight orders in all), viz. subdeacons, acolytes, exorcists, readers, doorkeepers: these were appointed by giving them some article required in their ministrations; thus the acolyte was given a linen bag, the receptacle then used for the consecrated bread (see p. 209), and the subdeacon a chalice (or a chalice and paten, with a water cruet and napkin)—his business being to keep these things in order. This was called the 'Tradition [i.e. delivery] of the Instruments'. The ordination of bishops, priests, and deacons was sharply distinguished from such admission to the minor orders by consisting of the laying on of hands. To this was added in the Gallican use the anointing of the priest's hands, after his ordination. In the Missal of Leofric, Bishop of Exeter (†1072), we find another ceremony, the blessing and giving of vestments—stoles for the deacons and chasubles to the priests --the chasuble, originally a garment common to lay-folk and clergy, being by this time mainly used by priests, though even at the present day it is still worn by deacons at certain seasons such as Lent.

In the 11th century a curious change began. The 'Tradition of the Instruments', which had been the way of appointing to the *minor* orders, and the distinctive mark of this appointment, came to be added to the three chief orders: to the priest was given a chalice with wine and a paten with a wafer; to the deacon, a Gospel Book. In an uncritical age this 'Tradition' —being a picturesque and striking ceremony—soon came to be looked upon as essential; and by 1439 we find a pope asserting that it is the 'matter', i.e. the outward sign, of the sacrament of Holy Order. This came to be accepted in the Roman Communion; and thus it was that some Roman Catholics have said that Anglican Orders were not valid, because this form of the 'Tradition of the Instruments' was dropped in the Second Prayer Book. In 1896 the Pope of Rome also found fault with our form of ordination to the priesthood, because the first four English Ordinals (1550, &c.) did not use the word 'priest' in immediate connexion with the imposition of hands. As a matter of fact, the services in all our five English Ordinals are called 'The Ordering of Deacons', 'The Ordering of Priests', and 'The Consecration of Bishops'; and the candidates in all our ordinals are presented 'to be admitted Deacons', 'to the Order of Priesthood', and 'to be consecrated Bishop'. The Pope's objection was thus rather thin, since the words were plainly used, and the intention (which he also called in question) perfectly definite. But the question was finally settled by the discovery only three years later, in Bishop Sarapion's Sacramentary, that he in the middle of the 4th century did not use the word 'priest' at all.

The first English Ordinal was not issued till 1550, the Sarum forms remaining in force for a year under the First Prayer Book. Cranmer and his colleagues acted wisely in reforming the confusion which had grown up in the Middle Ages; for in the Sarum books the primitive and Catholic ordination of a priest by laying on of hands—which we will call (1)—was followed by three additional ordinations, invented in the Middle Ages; (2) Anointing of the hands, (3) Tradition of the Instruments; and (4) a Second laying on of hands, with the words 'Receive the Holy Ghost', &c. In the Roman Use this is made worse; for the original imposition (no. 1) has actually disappeared, the bishop merely extending his hands, and only laying them on the candidate at no. 4.

The Reformers brought back the rites to the Scriptural

method, which was also that of Rome until the Middle Ages, by restoring to its proper place the imposition of hands; for this end they gave up the anointing (2), altered (3), and added the form of (4) to the original rite, (1). Otherwise they kept to the lines of the Sarum Pontifical, retaining the Presentation of the Candidates, Litany, Instruction, Bidding, *Veni Creator*, and Holy Communion. They retained also, in deference to current ideas, a modified form of the Tradition of the Instruments, the First Ordinal directing the bishop to give to each priest a Bible in one hand, and 'the Chalice or cup with the bread' in the other. In the Second Prayer Book the chalice and paten were omitted; and the giving of the Bible thus remains with us to-day, a ceremony not only eloquent for its own significance, but interesting also as a relic of that other Tradition which once took so large place in men's minds.

The changes in the Ordinal have been very slight, the chief being that in the third Question at the Ordination of Deacons. The deacon is asked in the English Ordinal, 'Do you unfeignedly believe all the Canonical Scriptures of the Old and New Testament?' This has been altered in the American, Canadian, and Scottish Prayer Books, the American form being, 'Are you persuaded that the Holy Scriptures contain all Doctrine required as necessary for eternal salvation through faith in Jesus Christ?' To which the candidate answers, 'I am so persuaded'.

SOME LANDMARKS IN THE HISTORY OF
PUBLIC WORSHIP

A.D.

Persia: Parthian Dynasty,
till 224

EMPERORS OF ROME

c. 29 After Pentecost the Gospel spreads
from Syria to Persia, Mesopotamia,
Asia Minor, North Africa, and
Rome (Acts 2: 9–10)

14 Tiberius

c. 40 Paul and Barnabas founding the
Church at Antioch.

37 Caligula

c. 48–56 Paul founding Churches in Asia
Minor and Greece

41–54 Claudius

c. 50–60 St. Paul's Epistles

54–68 Nero

c. 65 The Gospel according to St. Mark

68 Vespasian

c. 90 The Didachè

81–96 Domitian

c. 110 The Pastoral Epistles in their
present form

98–117 Trajan

c. 112 Pliny's letter about Christian worship

c. 155 St. Justin Martyr's description of
Baptism and Communion

136–61 Antoninus Pius

200 Christianity already in Great
Britain

193–211 Septimius
Severus

(224 *Persia:* Ardashir
founds Sasanian
dynasty)

Third century: National Churches in Armenia and Upper Mesopotamia

313 The Peace of the Church: toleration accorded in the Roman Empire

306–37 Constantine,
First Christian
Emperor

314 Three British Bishops attend
Council of Arles

325 Council of Nicæa (Nicene Creed,
in part). St. Athanasius (Bishop
of Alexandria, 326)

A.D.		EMPERORS OF ROME
c. 350	Earliest extant manuscripts of the Bible	
,,	Sacramentary of Sarapion	
374	St. Ambrose, Bishop of Milan, writes hymns	379–95 Theodosius
397	St. Ninian in Scotland	
398	St. Chrysostom, Bishop of Constantinople, introduces Litanies or out-door processions	Arcadius, Emperor of the East, Honorius of the West
c. 450	St. David and St. Patrick	———
c. 470	Mamertus, Bishop of Vienne (Rogation Litanies)	(*The Dark Ages*)
	500–600 Leonine Sacramentary	
	563 St. Columba leaves Ireland and lands in Iona (Gallican use)	

A.D.		ENGLISH KINGS
596	Conversion of Kent begun by St. Augustine, First Bishop of Canterbury (Roman use)	Æthelbert, King of Kent
		(638 *Persian Empire* conquered by Arabs)
c. 680	Athanasian Creed	
c. 735	The Gospels and Psalms translated into English by the Venerable Bede and others	
,,	Gelasian Sacramentary	
c. 800	Gregorian Sacramentary	
c. 900	The Psalter in Anglo-Saxon, the first fifty Psalms attributed, on fair evidence, to Alfred the Great	Alfred, King of Wessex

The Middle Ages

Most of our cathedrals and old parish churches were built between
the Norman Conquest, 1066, and the Wars of the Roses, 1450

A.D.		KINGS OF ENGLAND
1078	St. Osmund, Bishop of Salisbury	William the Conqueror
1217	Richard Poore, Bishop of Salisbury: Sarum Use written down	Henry III

A.D.		KINGS OF ENGLAND
1380	Wyclif. The Bible in Middle English	Richard II
1476	Caxton starts printing in England	Edward IV
		The Reformation
1533	English Church rejects Papal Supremacy	Henry VIII
1535	Coverdale's Bible	,,
1539	The Great Bible	,,
1543	Lessons in English	,,
1544	The Litany in English	,,
1548	The 'Order of the Communion' in English	Edward VI
,,	First Metrical Psalter	,,
1549	The First English Prayer Book	,,
1550	First English Ordinal	,,
1552	The Second English Prayer Book	,,
1559	The Third English Prayer Book	Elizabeth
1604	The Fourth English Prayer Book	James I
1611	The Authorized Version of the Bible	,,
1637	The Scottish Prayer Book published but rejected	Charles I
1662	The Present English Prayer Book	Charles II
1789	The First American Prayer Book	(George Washington, President U.S.A.)

(*For the other Prayer Books, &c., see pp.* 132–3)

A SHORT INDEX

REPRINTED BY LITHOGRAPHY
IN GREAT BRITAIN
BY JARROLD AND SONS LIMITED
NORWICH